University of South Carolina

Columbia, South Carolina

Written by Jessica Foster

Edited by Jaime Myers

Layout by Adam Burns

*Additional contributions by Omid Gohari,
Christina Koshzow, Chris Mason, Joey Rahimi
and Luke Skurman*

ISBN # 1-4274-0196-9
ISSN # 1552-1753
© Copyright 2006 College Prowler
All Rights Reserved
Printed in the U.S.A.
www.collegeprowler.com

Last updated 4/25/08

Special Thanks To: Babs Carryer, Andy Hannah, LaunchCyte, Tim O'Brien, Bob Sehlinger, Thomas Emerson, Andrew Skurman, Barbara Skurman, Bert Mann, Dave Lehman, Daniel Fayock, Chris Babyak, The Donald H. Jones Center for Entrepreneurship, Terry Slease, Jerry McGinnis, Bill Ecenberger, Idie McGinty, Kyle Russell, Jacque Zaremba, Larry Winderbaum, Roland Allen, Jon Reider, Team Evankovich, Lauren Varacalli, Abu Noaman, Mark Exler, Daniel Steinmeyer, Jared Cohon, Gabriela Oates, David Koegler, and Glen Meakem.

Bounce-Back Team: Brindy McNair, Patrick Augustine, and Joel Wallace.

College Prowler®
5001 Baum Blvd.
Suite 750
Pittsburgh, PA 15213

Phone: 1-800-290-2682
Fax: 1-800-772-4972
E-Mail: info@collegeprowler.com
Web Site: www.collegeprowler.com

How this all started...

When I was trying to find the perfect college, I used every resource that was available to me. I went online to visit school websites; I talked with my high school guidance counselor; I read book after book; I hired a private counselor. Sure, this was all very helpful, but nothing really told me what life was like at the schools I cared about. These sources weren't giving me enough information to be totally confident in my decision.

In all my research, there were only two ways to get the information I wanted.

The first was to physically visit the campuses and see if things were really how the brochures described them, but this was quite expensive and not always feasible. The second involved a missing ingredient: the students. Actually talking to a few students at those schools gave me a taste of the information that I needed so badly. The problem was that I wanted more but didn't have access to enough people.

In the end, I weighed my options and decided on a school that felt right and had a great academic reputation, but truth be told, the choice was still very much a crapshoot. I had done as much research as any other student, but was I 100 percent positive that I had picked the school of my dreams?

Absolutely not.

My dream in creating *College Prowler* was to build a resource that people can use with confidence. My own college search experience taught me the importance of gaining true insider insight; that's why the majority of this guide is composed of quotes from actual students. After all, shouldn't you hear about a school from the people who know it best?

I hope you enjoy reading this book as much as I've enjoyed putting it together. Tell me what you think when you get a chance. I'd love to hear your college selection stories.

Luke Skurman
CEO and Co-Founder
lukeskurman@collegeprowler.com

Welcome to College Prowler®

During the writing of College Prowler's guidebooks, we felt it was critical that our content was unbiased and unaffiliated with any college or university. We think it's important that our readers get honest information and a realistic impression of the student opinions on any campus—that's why if any aspect of a particular school is terrible, we (unlike a campus brochure) intend to publish it. While we do keep an eye out for the occasional extremist—the cheerleader or the cynic—we take pride in letting the students tell it like it is. We strive to create a book that's as representative as possible of each particular campus. Our books cover both the good and the bad, and whether the survey responses point to recurring trends or a variation in opinion, these sentiments are directly and proportionally expressed through our guides.

College Prowler guidebooks are in the hands of students throughout the entire process of their creation. Because you can't make student-written guides without the students, we have students at each campus who help write, randomly survey their peers, edit, layout, and perform accuracy checks on every book that we publish. From the very beginning, student writers gather the most up-to-date stats, facts, and inside information on their colleges. They fill each section with student quotes and summarize the findings in editorial reviews. In addition, each school receives a collection of letter grades (A through F) that reflect student opinion and help to represent contentment, prominence, or satisfaction for each of our 20 specific categories. Just as in grade school, the higher the mark the more content, more prominent, or more satisfied the students are with the particular category.

Once a book is written, additional students serve as editors and check for accuracy even more extensively. Our bounce-back team—a group of randomly selected students who have no involvement with the project—are asked to read over the material in order to help ensure that the book accurately expresses every aspect of the university and its students. This same process is applied to the 200-plus schools College Prowler currently covers. Each book is the result of endless student contributions, hundreds of pages of research and writing, and countless hours of hard work. All of this has led to the creation of a student information network that stretches across the nation to every school that we cover. It's no easy accomplishment, but it's the reason that our guides are such a great resource.

When reading our books and looking at our grades, keep in mind that every college is different and that the students who make up each school are not uniform—as a result, it is important to assess schools on a case-by-case basis. Because it's impossible to summarize an entire school with a single number or description, each book provides a dialogue, not a decision, that's made up of 20 different topics and hundreds of student quotes. In the end, we hope that this guide will serve as a valuable tool in your college selection process. Enjoy!

OMID GOHARI ○ CHRISTINA KOSHZOW ○ CHRIS MASON ○ JOEY RAHIMI ○ LUKE SKURMAN ○
The College Prowler Team

UNIVERSITY OF SOUTH CAROLINA

Table of Contents

By the Numbers............................ **1**

Academics **4**

Local Atmosphere **11**

Safety & Security **18**

Computers................................. **24**

Facilities..................................... **29**

Campus Dining.......................... **34**

Off-Campus Dining **43**

Campus Housing **50**

Off-Campus Housing................ **60**

Diversity..................................... **64**

Guys & Girls............................... **69**

Athletics..................................... **75**

Nightlife..................................... **82**

Greek Life **91**

Drug Scene................................ **97**

Campus Strictness **102**

Parking.....................................**106**

Transportation **111**

Weather...................................**117**

Report Card Summary............**121**

Overall Experience **122**

The Inside Scoop....................**126**

Finding a Job or Internship **130**

Alumni **132**

Student Organizations............**134**

The Best & Worst....................**139**

Visiting.....................................**141**

Words to Know........................**147**

Introduction from the Author

Pretty much everyone has heard of the University of South Carolina. Some people have heard of its nationally acclaimed international business school. Others have recognized its multi-million dollar facilities, some of which are among the largest and most technologically advanced in the state and the nation. While sports fans know it for its football, many others are simply aware of its long-standing presence as one of the original Southern public colleges, established in 1801. Even though the University of South Carolina was founded over 200 years ago, it is only now beginning to tap its full potential. While the school has experienced about as much growth as it can withstand in terms of student body population, it is currently undergoing an academic transformation from which the students are reaping the benefits.

So what exactly does it mean to be a Gamecock? It means living in the heart of South Carolina, in the capital city, surrounded by beaches to the east, mountains to the north, and the countryside a short drive away. The urban setting provides a multitude of internship opportunities and career options so that students can gain knowledge in the classroom and experience in the working world at the same time. Many don't forget the historical value of the college, which just barely survived the destruction of the Civil War and the turmoil of Reconstruction. Being a Gamecock means being part of a legacy of high-quality education that extends back through hundreds of years and continues to this day.

Now that you know a bit about the University of South Carolina, you probably want to know more about the everyday life of a Gamecock. This book will provide the answers to many of your questions about life at the University of South Carolina, coming straight from the source—the students. Hopefully it will guide you in making one of the most important decisions of your life. And if you do decide to join the thousands who have already chosen the University of South Carolina, be forewarned—being a Gamecock is not just a four-year experience, it is a lifelong journey.

Jessica Foster, Author
University of South Carolina

By the Numbers

General Information

University of South Carolina
Columbia, SC 29208

Control:
Public

Academic Calendar:
Semester

Religious Affiliation:
None

Founded:
1801

Web Site:
www.sc.edu

Main Phone:
(803) 777-7000

Student Body

**Full-Time
Undergraduates:**
17,247

**Part-Time
Undergraduates:**
1,580

**Total Male
Undergraduates:**
8,558

**Total Female
Undergraduates:**
10,269

Admissions

Overall Acceptance Rate:
59%

**Early Decision
Acceptance Rate:**
Not offered

**Early Action
Acceptance Rate:**
N/A

Regular Acceptance Rate:
59%

Total Applicants:
14,994

Total Acceptances:
8,908

Freshman Enrollment:
3,719

**Yield (% of admitted
students who actually enroll):**
42%

Early Action Deadline:
October 1

Early Action Notification:
December 20

Regular Decision Deadline:
December 1

**Regular Decision
Notification:**
March 15

Must-Reply-By Date:
May 1

**Applicants Placed on
Waiting List:**
270

**Applicants Accepting a
Place on Waiting List:**
70

**Students Enrolled from
Waiting List:**
34

**Transfer Applications
Received:**
3,577

**Transfer Applications
Accepted:**
2,055

Transfer Students Enrolled:
1,225

**Transfer Application
Acceptance Rate:**
57%

SAT I or ACT Required?
Yes, either

**SAT I Range
(25th–75th Percentile):**
1080–1280

**SAT I Verbal Range
(25th–75th Percentile):**
530–630

**SAT I Math Range
(25th–75th Percentile):**
550–650

**ACT Composite Range
(25th–75th Percentile):**
23–28

Retention Rate:
87%

**Top 10% of High
School Class:**
29%

**Common Application
Accepted?**
No

Supplemental Forms?
No

Application Fee:
$50

Admissions Phone:
(803) 777-7700
(800) 868-5872

Admissions E-Mail:
admissions-ugrad@sc.edu

Admissions Web Site:
www.sc.edu/admissions

Financial Information

In-State Tuition:
$7,946

Out-of-State Tuition:
$21,232

Room and Board:
$6,946

Books and Supplies:
$900

**Average Need-Based
Financial Aid Package
(including loans, work-study,
grants, and other sources):**
$10,558

**Students Who Applied
for Financial Aid:**
69%

**Applicants Who Received
Aid:**
68%

Financial Aid Forms Deadline:
April 1

Financial Aid Phone:
(803) 777-8134

Financial Aid E-Mail:
USCFAID@sc.edu

Financial Aid Web Site:
www.sc.edu/financialaid

Academics

The Lowdown On...
Academics

Degrees Awarded:
Associate
Bachelor's
Post-bachelor's certificate
Master's
Post-master's certificate
Doctorate
First professional

Most Popular Majors:
25.2% Business/marketing
9.6% Social sciences
8.3% Communications
6.6% Biological/life sciences
6.3% Psychology

➔

Undergraduate Schools:

Arnold School of Public Health

College of Arts and Sciences

College of Education

College of Engineering
and Computing

College of Hospitality, Retail, &
Sport Management

College of Mass
Communications and
Information Studies

College of Nursing

College of Pharmacy

College of Social Work

Moore School of Business

School of Music

Full-Time Faculty:
1,250

Faculty with Terminal Degree:
84%

Student-to-Faculty Ratio:
16:1

Average Course Load:
15 hours

Class Sizes:
Fewer than 20 Students: 46%
20 to 49 Students: 45%
50 or More Students: 9%

Graduation Rates:
Four-Year: 40%
Five-Year: 60%
Six-Year: 63%

Special Degree Options

Accelerated program, cooperative education program, cross-registration, distance learning, double major, dual enrollment, English as a Second Language (ESL), exchange student program (domestic), external degree program, honors program, independent study, interdisciplinary studies program (College of Hospitality, Retail, and Sport Management), internships, study abroad, teacher certification program, weekend college.

Also available: Alternative Spring Break, Dobson Volunteer Service Program, International Program for Students

AP Test Score Requirements
Possible credit for scores of 3, 4, or 5

Best Places to Study:

Thomas Cooper Library, Horseshoe, dorm study rooms

Academic Clubs
Academic Team, American Chemical Society, American Institute of Chemical Engineers, Anthropology Student Association, Carolina Debate, Comparative Literature Student Association, Criminal Justice Association, DMSB Doctoral Student Association, Geography Club, Geology Club, German Club, Health Law Society, Marine Science Graduate Society, Marine Science Undergraduate Society, Mock Trial Team, Psychology Graduate Student Association, Russian Club, Society for the Advancement of Chemical Sciences, Statistics Club, Undergraduate Political Science

Did You Know?

The University of South Carolina was ranked in a national academic survey as being the **best in the nation for its "Programs that Work"** for entering students. The International Business program for graduate students was ranked second in the nation.

White House Chief-of-Staff Andrew Card, Jr., Pulitzer Prize-winner Jim Hoagland, and Grammy Award-winning musicians Hootie and the Blowfish are among some of the University of South Carolina's **most notable alumni**.

What is an hour? At the University of South Carolina, **an hour usually refers to a credit**, and doesn't necessarily mean an hour of time. The amount of credit received for a class is measured in hours, and most classes are worth one or three credit hours.

Students Speak Out On...
Academics

"There is a spectrum. I've had miserably horrible teachers, and I've had ones that were interesting, witty, and incredibly gifted in their fields."

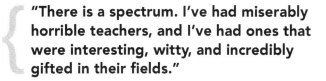 "Teachers are teachers. Everyone is different. It all **depends on what department** you are talking about. I only know theater faculty, and they're all great. I don't know very much about everyone else, but I haven't heard any horror stories yet."

Q "All of the teachers that I had thus far have been tremendous. They are willing to **meet with you and give you as much help as you need**. They will meet with you during their office hours or set up another time. I guess you could say the teachers are really good. They all really seem to care."

Q "USC has a diverse and **world-renowned faculty**. We have several colleges ranked in the nation."

Q "Some teachers are fantastic, and a few are terrible. Many are extremely intelligent and knowledgeable but just not very interesting. The key is to **do your research before signing up for classes**. Ask people from your major—they will tell you who to take and who not to take. That is always key. For your first semester, it won't make that much of a difference, but as you get deeper into your specific major, you'll really want to get into the best classes."

Q "It's really hard to say. When you get there, **the first semester you hardly know any of the teachers**, but by your second semester, you will hear who to take and not to take. Later on, it all depends on what major you are taking."

Q "I really like the professors; they're just fine here. You can always find the type of professor you want, but keep in mind, it's not high school anymore. They treat you fairly, in my opinion. USC is a big school, though, so there isn't always a lot of personal help unless your **classes have a graduate student teaching assistant** (TA)."

Q "A great help when going online to register for classes, or even just for seeing the grading system of teachers and classes, is *www.teacherreview.com*. Go to the Web site and go to 'South Carolina' then to 'University of South Carolina (Columbia)' and then click on 'professors.' It will give you an alphabetical listing of professors, each with information from students who have had that specific professor at USC. They go on the site and give them grades with explanations. It's very helpful!"

Q "Teachers are normal. You get the **stuffy old professors** who have been lecturing the same way for years, and you get the new ones that are willing to try new things. Classes are all right. However, I haven't really begun any classes related to my major so I'm not too interested in the general classes I'm currently taking."

Q "I find most classes interesting, but there are a few that just go on and on. I also find that in some classes, rather than being taught new things, I feel like **the professors are just using their position to enforce their opinions** on their students."

Q "Most of the teachers are really nice, but you don't really get to know them too well because **many of the classes are so big**."

Q "The professors at the University of South Carolina vary in quality from the course to the actual course size. I find that the English and foreign language department faculty are very helpful in the sense that **they truly care and are willing to spend outside class time** in order to better students' understanding of the material. Teachers' attitudes and zeal for teaching help make the coursework seem worthwhile and satisfying. As for the math and science department faculty, because of the large class size, it seems as if the teachers are disconnected and uninterested in the achievement of their students. There are few that really seem concerned with the students' progress."

Q "I've liked most of my teachers. I was interested in most of the honors classes that I took, but I didn't really like the non-honors classes. Also, **discussion-based classes are 10 times better than lecture classes**."

The College Prowler Take On...
Academics

It seems impossible for students to categorize the teachers at here as good or bad. The difficulty is that the students have a range of preferences when it comes to teaching methods. While some think that the best teachers are the ones that give them an easy A, others prefer a challenge. Some prefer a lecture format and others find a Socratic-style question-and-answer session more stimulating. There are all kinds of teachers with varying teaching methods and levels of personal involvement with the students. Academic advisers are helpful when trying to find out information about particular teachers, but sometimes students are forced to rely on word of mouth to find out what teachers will best meet their needs.

The Honors College provides academic opportunities for students who qualify, offering challenging courses with the best teachers, seminars, and perks such as better on-campus housing. Students can choose to be a part of one of the USC's nationally-ranked programs like international business, public relations, and advertising. This is an exciting time to be attending the University of South Carolina because of the growth and changes. Ultimately, the education you receive here depends on the effort you put forth, but the means of obtaining an excellent education is definitely there for those who desire to take advantage.

B

The College Prowler® Grade on
Academics: B

A high Academics grade generally indicates that professors are knowledgeable, accessible, and genuinely interested in their students' welfare. Other determining factors include class size, how well professors communicate, and whether or not classes are engaging.

Local Atmosphere

The Lowdown On...
Local Atmosphere

Region:
Southeast

City, State:
Columbia, SC

Setting:
Urban

Distance from Charleston:
2 hours

Distance from Atlanta:
3.5 hours

Points of Interest:
Columbia Museum of Art
Downtown Columbia
Frankie's Fun Park
Koger Center for the Performing Arts
Lake Murray
McKissick Museum
Riverbanks Zoo
Sesquicentennial State Park

➜

Shopping Malls:

Columbia Place
Columbiana Centre
Richland Mall

Movie Theaters:

AMC Dutch Square 14
800 Bush River Rd., Columbia
(803) 750-3576

Carmike 14
122 Afton Ct., Columbia
(803) 781-3067

Columbiana Grande
1250 Bower Pkwy., Columbia
(803) 407-9898

Columbia Place 8
7201 Two Notch Rd., Columbia
(803) 788-7664

(Movie Theaters, continued)

Movies at Polo Road
9700 Two Notch Rd., Columbia
(803) 788-7818

Nickelodeon Theatre
937 Main St., Columbia
(803) 254-3433

Pastime Pavilion 8
929 North Lake Dr., Lexington
(803) 951-3603

Regal Columbia Cinema 7
3400 Forest Dr., Columbia
(803) 790-9001

Major Sports Teams:

Columbia Bombers (baseball)
Columbia Inferno (hockey)

City Web Sites

www.columbiasc.net
www.columbiasouthcarolina.com

Did You Know?

5 Fun Facts about Columbia:

- Columbia is where the **first American library**, housed in a separate building, was built in 1840 on the University of South Carolina campus.

- Every summer, thousands of Purple Martins return to Bomb Island on Lake Murray to roost. This island has been declared a **bird sanctuary**, and many like to watch the birds return to the island each day around sunset.

- At **Riverbanks Zoological Park**, more than 2,000 animals thrive in recreated habitats without cages or bars.

- The Carolina Center in Columbia has **attracted acts such as Jimmy Buffett, Bruce Springsteen**, and President George W. Bush.

- The **Strom Thurmond Fitness and Wellness Center** features state-of-the-art equipment and a 52-foot climbing wall.

Famous People from Columbia:

Whispering Bill Anderson (Singer)

James Mark Baldwin (Psychologist)

Joseph H. Burckhalter (Inventor)

Alex English (Basketball player)

Local Slang:

Coke – Refers to any kind of soda.

Sketch – Suspicious or unusual.

Straight – Okay or all right.

Ya'll – You all.

Students Speak Out On...
Local Atmosphere

{ **"The atmosphere is great at Carolina. There is a lot to do on campus, and if you want to go off campus, there is plenty to do for everyone."**

Q "Columbia is a medium-sized city with well over 100,000 in the metro area. There is a women's college (Columbia College) and two small African American colleges in town. Clemson University, our bitter rival, is about 100 miles northwest of us in a tiny little town. The College of Charleston, another large university, is 90 miles to the east. Charlotte, North Carolina is 70 miles north on the freeway, and Atlanta is a three-hour drive. Charleston, South Carolina may be **the most beautiful and historic town in the country** and well worth many trips."

Q "This is the South. The biggest adjustment is a cultural one. The **people are incredibly warm and friendly** (almost suspiciously so to an outsider), and you have to deal with the eccentricities and the sometimes backwards thinking. It is pretty much politically conservative and religious, although it's less so on campus."

Q "I love Columbia! It's a great place, and we are only **two hours from the mountains and two hours from the beach**! Charleston is a great place to go because the College of Charleston (a huge party school) and the Citadel (a military-type school with hot guys) are about two hours away! There aren't any other big universities around except Clemson, which is about two and a half hours away from here."

Q "Stay away from Two Notch Road and North Main Street, especially at night. Drugs and prostitution are horrible there, as well as any side of town that looks especially dirty. Surprisingly, **Columbia itself is a very clean city** for its size, as compared to New York and Atlanta. It's nowhere near as big as those cities, but it is very neat and clean. It doesn't get very dirty here, except in the shifty side of town. The campus at night is fairly safe to walk around, and the USC police are always on patrol. There are other universities in Columbia, but none really close to the USC area. USC is the heart of downtown Columbia, and the others are on the fringes of town."

Q "If you like city life, this is the university for you. If not, go somewhere out in the country. **It is a busy campus**. There are relaxing locations on campus such as the Horseshoe, but other than that, it is a 'go, go, go' atmosphere. Columbia is very open and spread out. There are lots of things to do during the day. Things to visit are the state museum and Riverbank Zoo."

Q "The atmosphere in Columbia is **very laid-back and kind**. People aren't in a hurry here. Everything moves pretty slowly. I'd definitely visit the museum, Lake Murray, and the zoo. The zoo here is very neat, and is one of the nicest in the United States. I can't really think of anything to stay away from except for the neighborhood called Olympia."

Q "Since South Carolina is one of the original slave states, there are different cities you can visit that still have historical houses and things for you to look at. In Columbia, there's a pretty cool museum. And downtown **Columbia has historic houses**."

Q "There are other universities, but USC is so big that we never acknowledge them. If you need something to do, there is the state capitol, lots of museums, football (of course), malls, lots of bars, and the coliseum. It is a very **big college town with lots of politicians around**."

Q "We are **very close to a military base** that has a basic-training base for the army, so there are a lot of military people around. We have a big tech school near us called Midlands Tech College, and there are a few other smaller campuses such as Benedict College nearby. There is a zoo close by, too. You have to hit the city of Charleston and Myrtle Beach. The cities are awesome, very fun, and about two hours away."

Q "Columbia is a fairly nice-sized city. Here, you have the feel of a big city, but with the location of the campus, you are away from most of the business that comes along with that. I know of at least **seven different colleges** located here, but I'm sure there are more, so there are plenty of college students running around. Here, we have a few malls, a really nice zoo, the state museum, and a river, along with other things to keep you busy."

Q "Columbia, South Carolina is a small city in comparison to many other college towns, but it has its pluses. The area has many places to relax and chill out, such as coffee shops and dance clubs. I highly recommend having an awareness of certain hangouts. Underage college students should be careful around Five Points and the Vista if they opt to drink or surround themselves with people that may drink. What to visit? Columbia is only an hour and a half away from Charleston and the Blue Ridge Mountains. So, **any sort of atmosphere you'd like is a short distance** away if you can't find it in Columbia."

Q "Columbia is a great place. It's a **decent-sized city, but it's still really friendly with lots of green space**. I think both Benedict and Allen University are in Columbia also, but they are on the other side of town. There are lots of great places in Columbia for everybody."

The College Prowler Take On...
Local Atmosphere

Located in the heart of Columbia, many students are delighted by the mix of Southern charm on campus and the fast pace of the urban setting. The campus grounds are scattered with gorgeous greenery and secluded gardens. USC also harbors a vast array of historical treasures. On campus, students are able to visit McKissick Museum, which hosts art shows and collections featuring Southern culture. The Koger Center hosts fine musical, theatrical, and dance productions. Being in the South and smack in the middle of the "Bible belt," there is a lot of conservative thinking. This appeals to some and frustrates others. Many are also involved in the political scene. Students make their voices heard on issues such as budget cuts, which threatened to take away scholarship money, and the war in Iraq.

And of course, you absolutely cannot attend the University of South Carolina without going to see the monkeys (and I'm not talking about the ones in the state house). Riverbanks Zoo, the State Museum, and Lake Murray are favorites among students. If you're willing to travel a bit, Charleston, Myrtle Beach, Atlanta, and the Blue Ridge Mountains are all within a few hours. The Southern atmosphere, the urban setting, and the variety of activities in the area combine to make the atmosphere at USC ideal for many students.

The College Prowler® Grade on
Local Atmosphere: B+

A high Local Atmosphere grade indicates that the area surrounding campus is safe and scenic. Other factors include nearby attractions, proximity to other schools, and the town's attitude toward students

Safety & Security

The Lowdown On...
Safety & Security

Number of USC Police:
32

Police Phone:
(803) 777-4215

Safety Services:
24-Hour Help Line
Emergency Call-Boxes
Escort Services
Rape Aggression Defense
Shuttle System

Health Services:
Basic Medicine
Blood Pressure Checks
Cholesterol Screenings
Counseling
STD Testing
Women's Care Clinic

Health Center Office Hours

Monday–Saturday 8 a.m.–5 p.m.
Sundays (for urgent conditions only) 4 p.m.–8 p.m.

Did You Know?

Once the button on an emergency call-box has been pushed, the USC Police Department typically has **an officer on the scene in less than one minute**.

Students Speak Out On...
Safety & Security

> "At every location on campus, there is a call-box within view. If anything ever happens, you run to one and hit a button. A big, blue light starts flashing soon after, and the police are there within minutes."

Q "Security on campus is pretty good. We have campus police, and you see them riding around on their bikes or in the cars, but unfortunately, there is crime everywhere. I think that the security does all they possibly can. Most of the **dorms have security officers at the desk**, and you have to sign your male guest in; female guests have to be signed in after 8 p.m."

Q "**Common sense needs to be used**. You can't go walking alone at 3 a.m. and expect your safety to be as it would earlier in the evening."

Q "I've never had any problems, but there are some incidents that occur every once in a while. Mostly everything is pretty well lit. The **dorms are also pretty safe**, although some of the freshman ones are pretty slack on who can come in and whatnot."

Q "As a guy, I am not as security conscious as a girl might be, but I have been told by my female friends that they feel very safe here. We have an **incredibly low crime rate for a major campus**, and they seem to do a really good job in this area. In my three years here, I have yet to meet anyone who has had a negative experience in this respect."

Q "USC has its **own private police force, the USCPD**, which is very good (except when they're pulling you over to give you a speeding ticket). There are usually patrol cars driving around everywhere, and if you are walking around at night, because it is a pretty big campus, you can call campus security, and they will drive you around."

Q "The University Police Department does a very good job. There are **call-boxes set up all over campus in the case of an emergency**. All you would have to do is press the button. The call-box has a speaker so that they can hear what is going on for up to 90 feet from the box. They have said that it takes approximately one minute and 15 seconds for them to be on the scene. Also, if you don't feel safe walking across campus at night for some reason, you can call them and they will pick you up and give you a ride to wherever you need to go, or they'll walk with you."

Q "Security is fine, just don't be stupid and think you're invincible just because you're in college and on your own—stay in groups after dark. Use your intuition and common sense. If something doesn't feel right, it usually isn't. And there are these call-boxes all around campus that you can call, even if it's not an emergency. They'll **send an escort over if you ask**, even if there's no emergency."

Q "USC has a wonderful security program. I feel far safer around campus than I do anywhere else in the United States. There are tons of emergency boxes spread across campus that allow anyone to access help from police at any given time. Just like at any college, I recommend you always be on the watch out. But as for USC, any individual can feel assured that **USC's high-quality certified staff is working for the students'** best interest."

Q "USC has its own police department that patrols, and there are call-boxes are all around campus. **Central campus is pretty safe**, but I wouldn't walk around the outer edges of it by myself."

Q "I generally feel pretty safe on campus. I still like to stay in areas that have at least some light, but **there hasn't been a time when I have felt afraid** to walk around on campus alone."

The College Prowler Take On...
Safety & Security

Being in the middle of a city, there are dangerous people. If students are not careful, they can find themselves in a dangerous situation. However, the University provides a number of services to ensure safety. In addition to the city police force, the USC Police Department (USCPD) patrol campus 24 hours a day. The call-boxes placed throughout campus allow students fast access to the USCPD in an emergency situation. There is also an escort service that operates five nights a week between 8 p.m. and 12 a.m. if students feel they are in an unsafe situation.

In spite of the tight security on campus, stuff still happens. Students can often avoid these situations if they practice simple safety precautions. Students are warned not to go out alone when it's dark, and some students opt to carry pepper spray, just in case. It's also helpful to have a cell phone in case you want to call the police or escort service, but are not close to a call-box. And to avoid theft, it's always a good idea to make sure that your dorm room and your car are locked, and that you leave valuable possessions out of sight. In general, the safety of students is in their own hands because most situations can be avoided by employing the proper safety precautions.

B

The College Prowler® Grade on

Safety & Security: B

A high grade in Safety & Security means that students generally feel safe, campus police are visible, blue-light phones and escort services are readily available, and safety precautions are not overly necessary.

Computers

The Lowdown On...
Computers

High-Speed Network?
Yes

Wireless Network?
Yes

Number of Labs:
8

Number of Computers:
More than 200 in Thomas Cooper Library and 16 in each dorm lab

Operating Systems:
Mac (anything above 9.3 recommended)
PC (Windows XP Pro or 2000+ recommended)
UNIX

Free Software

McAfee Virus Scan, Virex

24-Hour Labs

Bates, Patterson, the Towers, Columbia Hall

Charge to Print?

Varies

Did You Know?

Computer Services offers **free software training** classes for students.

Long distance and voice mail services are also available to students through Computer Services by visiting *www.csd.sc.edu*.

Students Speak Out On...
Computers

"I definitely recommend bringing your own computer because most of the time the labs are full. Although the labs are nice and beneficial, it's so much better having your own computer."

Q "The computer network here is great; it almost never goes down. We also have really good computer labs that are never full. You can always have access to a computer when you need it. If you are living on campus, I would recommend bringing your own computer just for the sake of convenience. It is great to just **plug in and download music in your own room**. But, at the same time, you can also get by without it."

Q "Definitely bring your computer. I think you need to have one in your room because you will always want to be on the Internet, and sometimes you just won't feel like going to the computer lab. Computer labs aren't bad, but I really **like having my own computer because it is easier** and just more convenient."

Q "The system is a really good one, and computer services on campus are very good. They help out so much! The **system is very fast**; it's an Ethernet connection—I love it. I really do. I don't think the labs are always full. Most kids at USC have their own computers, and the library is very well-equipped with them, so I don't think computers would be a problem. But, it would probably be better if you have your own computer and register it through the school when you get here. It would be a lot easier for you."

Q "Bring your own computer! **My computer is like my best friend**. I can't do anything without it. I usually use it mainly for IM and downloading music. The network is ridiculously fast."

Q "I have my own computer, and it is good to have your own. We have **Internet connections in the dorm rooms**. You just have to get an Ethernet card put into your computer. The computer labs aren't always crowded, and you should usually be able to find an empty computer there. The library also has a lot of computers for use."

Q "There's a **huge computer lab at the campus library**, which is rarely ever completely full, unless it's at exam time and everyone is rushing to do their papers. You may want to bring your own PC just for convenience purposes."

Q "Computer labs may be crowded, but there's usually an open terminal somewhere because there are so many computers in each lab. Bring your own computer anyway, because it really sucks to be trekking across campus at 2 a.m. trying to print out a report due that morning. The network isn't one of the fastest—I've seen colleges that have connections so fast you can download the entire Internet by the time you get out of the shower in the morning, but it's decent. It crashes every once in a while, and that can be really annoying when a teacher **requires homework posted online**. But for the most part, it's all right."

Q "It isn't exactly necessary for a student to bring their own computer to USC. However, because of convenience, if it is within one's means, I would highly recommend it. USC has a **great network and plenty of computer labs**."

Q "I had my own computer, but when it broke one time, I used the computer lab, and it was never crowded, but you do have to be **patient with the printers**. With so many people using them, they tend to break."

The College Prowler Take On...
Computers

Students at USC rely heavily on computers both in and out of the classroom. Computers are required for writing papers, doing research on the Internet, creating projects, and checking homework assignments and grades online through Blackboard. Students also use USC's Visual Information Processing (VIP) system online to register for classes and pay their tuition. The computer labs on campus provide ample resources for students. However, many students find it more convenient to have their own computer for downloading music, chatting with friends, and simply because they can use it any time without having to walk across campus.

The Internet connection is much better than what many students are used to. There is a high-speed Ethernet connection, and students also have the option of setting up a wireless connection with Computer Services. The network occasionally experiences problems, but there are generally few and far between. Computer Services also provides in-room and over-the-phone assistance with your computer, in case you have problems or questions. Whether you decide to bring your own computer or use the University facilities, you will find the technological resources easily-accessible and of high quality.

B+

The College Prowler® Grade on
Computers: B+

A high grade in Computers designates that computer labs are available, the computer network is easily accessible, and the campus' computing technology is up-to-date.

Facilities

The Lowdown On...
Facilities

Student Center:
The Russell House
University Union

Athletic Center:
Blatt PE Center
Strom Thurmond Wellness
and Fitness Center

Libraries:
8

Campus Size:
358 acres

Popular Places to Chill:
Cool Beans coffee shop
The Horseshoe
The Russell House
University Union

What Is There to Do on Campus?

Whether you want to get buff at the gym, watch a fine theatrical production, read a book, grab some grub, see a free movie in the student center, or attend a game at the Carolina Center, there is always plenty to do on campus.

Movie Theater on Campus?

Yes, in the Russell House University Union

Bar on Campus?

No

Coffeehouse on Campus?

No, but Cool Beans is less than a block from the Horseshoe on College Street.

Favorite Things to Do?

Many students enjoy going to see flicks for free at the Russell House, which are usually playing several nights a week. Similarly, there is almost always a theatrical production showing at Longstreet Theater or Drayton Hall, which draw rather large crowds. *The Crucible*, *The Vagina Monologues*, and *The Shape of Things* are a few examples of the plays that received a lot of publicity. The University also hosts Late Night Carolina every semester, where students can get free food, watch movies, and participate in games and other activities like making their own music videos or doing arts and crafts. If music is your thing, the Koger Center hosts bands and orchestras, as well as dance and theatrical performances. The new gym has also given students more incentive to get in shape. There is always a big crowd lifting weights, swimming, running, playing basketball or racquetball, or climbing the 52-foot climbing wall. Whether you are in the mood for burning some energy or getting some rest and relaxation, the facilities at the University of South Carolina provide several options for students when they want to get out of their dorms.

Students Speak Out On...
Facilities

"We have a $70 million PE center. We also built a coliseum for our basketball teams that brings great events and concerts to the University. Everything else is excellent."

Q "The University just finished a huge fundraising drive in order to make the facilities here top-notch. The computer centers here are excellent, and the **athletic facilities are also top-of-the-line**. I heard they are installing a Jumbotron screen. The only thing that I think needs to be updated is the student center—it's not bad, just average."

Q "There are **movies that run all week in the theater in the student union**. There are always presentations somewhere and music shows in the Koger Center. We have the Coliseum, where a minor league hockey team plays on campus."

Q "The Russell House is the student union, and there's quite a lot to do there—a lot goes on there. Often, they show free movies at the Russell House Theater before they even come out, and **there's always free fun stuff to do**."

Q "The campus is really nice. **We have a Greek village (fraternity and sorority houses)**, and they recently finished a new sports arena for the basketball team (the hockey team gets the old one), a new student and intramural sports facility, and two new apartment-style upperclassman dorms."

Q "I think that the new gym is the largest workout gym in the whole state; it also **has an Olympic-sized pool**! The student center has restaurants, and lots of people are always there. We have a great football stadium. A Greek village was built, and we have a new basketball arena."

Q "They just **opened up the Strom Thurmond Center**, and a one-word description would be: nice."

Q "Campus facilities at USC are amazing. The recreational center is a phenomenon. Its up-to-date equipment and technology make it easy for any student to come and go at their own convenience. **Academic tutoring is another one of USC's perks**. There, you can find a variety of free help, whether it's with the writing center or the math labs that are open at a vast variety of times."

Q "The new gym is really nice and has something for everyone to enjoy. The library has so many resources for students to use. The student center is great because it has a **cafeteria, a movie theater, conference rooms**, and other things that are good to have on campus."

Q "I would have to **rate the facilities average**; they aren't that bad. There could be improvements, but I think you are going to find room for improvement at any university."

The College Prowler Take On...
Facilities

With all of the improvements that have been made on campus, students seem to be very satisfied overall. The Strom Thurmond Wellness and Fitness Center houses five basketball courts, an indoor and outdoor pool, an indoor track, a climbing wall, and strength training equipment. Students really enjoy taking advantage of the long hours and brand new equipment in this multi-million-dollar facility. There is also the Carolina Center, which is the largest arena in the state, seating 18,000 and featuring a state-of-the-art sound system and a four-sided scoreboard.

The Russell House University Union is where students get food, check their mail, get tickets for sporting events, watch movies, and attend group events. While many get tired of the food, it too has been undergoing renovations to expand the food court selection. It may be termed average in comparison with some of USC's other facilities, but it seems to suffice the needs of students. The Thomas Cooper Library contains millions of volumes and microforms and over 200 computers. In addition, USC has been working to create a program that would allow students to access resources at all of the university libraries throughout the state.

The College Prowler® Grade on

Facilities: A-

A high Facilities grade indicates that the campus is aesthetically pleasing and well-maintained; facilities are state-of-the-art, and libraries are exceptional. Other determining factors include the quality of both athletic and student centers and an abundance of things to do on campus.

Campus
Dining

The Lowdown On...
Campus Dining

Freshman Meal Plan Requirement?

Yes

Meal Plan Average Cost:

$1,034 per semester

Places to Grab a Bite with Your Meal Plan:

Bates Carolina Diner

Food: Buffet

Location: Bates House

Hours: Monday–Thursday
7 a.m.–10 a.m., 11 a.m.–1 p.m.,
5 p.m.–12 a.m.,
Friday 7 a.m.–10 a.m.,
5 p.m.–6:30 p.m., Saturday–
Sunday 11 a.m.–1 p.m.,
5 p.m.–6:30 p.m.

Burger King

Food: American

Location: The Russell House University Union

Hours: Monday–Thursday 8:30 a.m.–10 p.m., Friday 8:30 a.m.–9 p.m., Sunday 12 p.m.–9 p.m.

Chick-fil-A

Food: American

Location: The Russell House University Union

Hours: Monday–Friday 10:30 a.m.–10 p.m., Saturday 12 p.m.–9 p.m.

The Coffee Cup

Food: Coffee, pastries

Location: The Russell House University Union

Hours: Monday–Thursday 7:30 a.m.–5 p.m., Friday 7:30 a.m.–3 p.m.

Cooper's Corner

Food: Grab-and-go sandwiches, salads

Location: Thomas Cooper Library

Hours: Monday–Wednesday 9 a.m.–9 p.m., Thursday– Friday 9 a.m.–3 p.m.

Einstein Bros. Bagels

Food: Bagels, coffee

Location: The Russell House University Union

Hours: Monday–Friday 7:30 a.m.–3:30 p.m., Saturday– Sunday 9 a.m.–2:30 p.m.

Express Café

Food: Grab-and-go sandwiches, salads

Location: Law Center

Hours: Monday–Thursday 7:30 a.m.–1:30 p.m.

Fast Break

Food: Grab-and-go sandwiches, chili

Location: Carolina Coliseum

Hours: Monday–Thursday 7:30 a.m.–4 p.m., Friday 7:30 a.m.–3 p.m.

Gibbes Court

Food: Deli, pizza station, hot line

Location: Capstone Residence Hall

Hours: Monday–Thursday 7 a.m.–10 p.m., Friday 7 a.m.–7 p.m., Saturday 11 a.m.–7 p.m., Sunday 11 a.m.–9 p.m.

Grand Market Place

Food: Salad bar, deli, International station, sushi bar, grill, vegetarian station, bakery, hot line

Location: The Russell House University Union

Hours: Monday–Thursday 7 a.m.–9 p.m., Friday 7 a.m.–8 p.m., Saturday 9 a.m.–8 p.m., Sunday 9 a.m.–9 p.m.

Jazzman's Café

Food: Coffee, bakery and grab-and-go items

Location: BA Building and on Hampton Street

Hours: (BA) Monday–Thursday 7:30 a.m.–5 p.m., Friday 7:30 a.m.–2 p.m.

(HS) Monday–Friday 7:30 a.m.–2:30 p.m.

Mein Bowl

Food: Asian

Location: The Russell House University Union

Hours: Monday–Thursday 11 a.m.–2 p.m., 5 p.m.–8 p.m., Friday 11 a.m.–2 p.m.

Pandini's

Food: Italian

Location: The Russell House University Union

Hours: Sunday–Thursday 11 a.m.–10 p.m., Friday 11 a.m.–7 p.m.

The Patio Café

Food: Buffet

Location: Patterson Hall

Hours: Monday–Thursday 7 a.m.–10 p.m., Friday 7 a.m.–7 p.m., Saturday 11 a.m.–7 p.m., Sunday 11 a.m.–9 p.m.

Pizza Hut

Food: Pizza, Italian

Location: The Russell House University Union

(Pizza Hut, continued)

Hours: Monday–Thursday 11 a.m.–12 a.m., Friday 11 a.m.–3 p.m.

Pump Bar

Food: Fitness bar

Location: Wellness Center

Hours: Monday–Thursday 8 a.m.–5 p.m., Friday 8 a.m.–4 p.m.

Sidewalk Café

Food: Grab-and-go sandwiches, salads

Location: Humanities Building

Hours: Monday–Thursday 7:30 a.m.–3:30 p.m., Friday 7:30 a.m.–2:30 p.m.

Starbucks

Food: Coffee, pastries

Location: The Russell House University Union

Hours: Monday–Thursday 7:30 a.m.–5 p.m., Friday 7:30 a.m.–3 p.m.

Sub Connection

Food: Sub sandwiches

Location: The Russell House University Union

Hours: Monday–Thursday 11 a.m.–11 p.m., Friday 11 a.m.–4 p.m.

Taco Bell Express

Food: Mexican

Location: The Russell House University Union

Hours: Monday–Thursday 11 a.m.–12 a.m., Friday 11 a.m.–3 p.m., Saturday 12 p.m.–10 p.m.

Zia Juice

Food: Smoothie bar

Location: The Russell House University Union

Hours: Monday–Thursday 10 a.m.–10 p.m., Friday 10 a.m.–4 p.m.

24-Hour On-Campus Dining?

No

Student Favorites:

The Grand Market Place

Off-Campus Places to Use Your Meal Plan:

See "Did You Know?" on page 38.

Other Options:

There are small trolley cars located around campus called Carolina Fast Track that are not included under the meal plan, but they do take cash cards and are a convenient way for students to grab a drink or a bite to eat.

Did You Know?

The University of South Carolina **offers a Five Points Meal Plan**, which allows students to eat at many of their favorite restaurants off campus and acts like a debit card so that you only pay for what you eat. Participating restaurants include:

Adriana's
721 Saluda Ave.
(803) 799-7595

Andy's Deli
2005 Greene St.
(803) 799-2639

Burger King
10030 Two Notch Rd.
(803) 788-0003

Carolina Bagel
925 Sumter St.
(803) 799-6676

Dapper Don's (Gambino's)
2009 Greene St.
(803) 252-6700

Domino's
1124 Devine St.
(803) 256-8151

Groucho's Deli
611 Harden St.
(803) 799-5708

Hannah Jane's
2020 Devine St.
(803) 256-0428

Hardee's
901 Harden St.
(803) 254-9161

Jammin Java
1530 Main St.
(803) 254-5282

Just Fresh
817 Harden St.
(803) 929-6681

The Pita Pit
2002 Greene St.
(803) 799-4557

Pizza Hut
617 Main St.
(803) 799-5036

Zorba's Greek Restaurant
6169 Saint Andrews Rd.
(803) 772-4617

Students Speak Out On...
Campus Dining

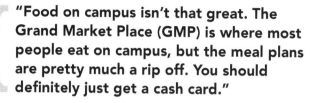

"Food on campus isn't that great. The Grand Market Place (GMP) is where most people eat on campus, but the meal plans are pretty much a rip off. You should definitely just get a cash card."

Q "I think the food on campus is above average. I don't mind it at all, but like everything else in life, you sometimes get tired of it and need a change. The best place to eat on campus is the Grand Market Place (GMP or the Gimp). The Gimp is located inside our student union. There you have a variety of choices from salads to something similar to a home-cooked meal. The only problem with the Gimp is that **they sometimes like to rip you off on prices**. Upstairs in the Russell House (student union), you have Taco Bell, Chick-fil-A, and Pizza Hut. There are also some more restaurants downstairs in the Russell House. A lot of people like the Patio Café, which is located inside one of the freshman girl dorms."

Q "I love the food! There are like **20 different places** to eat on campus. You hardly ever get tired of it. And they have this thing where you can eat at a bunch of off-campus restaurants as well, like Groucho's (my personal favorite), Zorba's, Pita Pit, Burger King, Hardee's, Andy's Deli, and many sit-down restaurants."

Q "I love eating on campus. It's so convenient, and there's a wide variety of food. Be sure to visit the **GMP for Chicken Finger Wednesday** and go to Pandini's! Such good food!"

Q "The food is decent. **A few dorms have cafeterias** in them, and right now on campus, there is a Chick-fil-A, Taco Bell, Pizza Hut, and the Grand Market Place. The Grand Market Place has a variety of foods like salads, a deli, a wok, hamburgers, and more. And they have recently extended the food plan to include Five Points. Five Points has different restaurants, bars, stores, and all sorts of things. And it's very close to the campus."

Q "There is great food! We have main restaurant chains, and we also have many cafeterias with **numerous buffet lines** with things like pasta, stir-fry, salads, hamburgers, chicken, subs, and anything you want—it's available. I love the food. There is great diversity and ample quality!"

Q "Food on campus ranges from average to good. It's not fantastic, but it's not bad either. The main student union in the middle of campus contains **everything from greasy fast food to a better-than-average cafeteria**, a good sub shop, and an average veggie place."

Q "The food is all right. It's better than some cafeteria food. The GMP has decent food, though toward the end of the year, it gets really old (or perhaps I was just yearning for a home-cooked meal). **Patterson has a buffet-style restaurant called the Patio**, which is really nice when you're hungry. There are a few lunch places on the way to some classes that are all right."

Q "The food on campus is really good. There is so much variety that **it is impossible to get tired of the food**. I love the Patio because it is all-you-can-eat and it was at the bottom of my dorm building last year. Bates Dining Hall was good because it was fancier, and it didn't feel like a cafeteria. The Sidewalk Café and Jazzman's were great, too, because they were a quick way to get a drink or grab some food."

Q "The food is not bad for being campus food. It is **overpriced for what you receive**, though. When all else fails, the Grand Market Place (GMP) is the place to go because it has a little bit of everything with its buffet-style facilities."

Q "If you want variety, then USC has it. A meal plan can provide a lot for any student. From the buffet style at the Patio to the Italian cuisine in Pandini's, **USC offers a variety of quality food**."

The College Prowler Take On...
Campus Dining

Chicken Finger Wednesday! Yes, USC students do get excited about their chicken fingers. But if for some reason chicken fingers don't tantalize your taste buds, there are plenty of other options. The Russell House University Union has the biggest variety of food options. It houses an Italian cuisine restaurant, a sub place, a juice bar, several fast food restaurants, and the Grand Market Place (affectionately called the Gimp). It offers salads, sandwiches, stir-fry, and home-style meals. Some of the dorm buildings, such as Capstone, Patterson, and Bates have their own cafeterias. On top of this, there are several grab-and-go places around campus where students can grab a bite on their way to or from class.

Students generally seem to rate the food on campus anywhere from average to good. The main complaint is that the it gets old after a while, which is understandable when you're eating campus food anywhere from 10–21 times a week. However, with all of the options available, it seems hard to believe that a student would be unable to find something that he or she likes. USC has a variety of food for all different tastes, from the health buff to the junk food junkie. It may not be your mom's home-cooking, but for campus food, most students find it pretty tasty.

The College Prowler® Grade on
Campus Dining: A-

Our grade on Campus Dining addresses the quality of both school-owned dining halls and independent on-campus restaurants, as well as the price, availability, and variety of food.

Off-Campus Dining

The Lowdown On...
Off-Campus Dining

Restaurant Prowler:
Popular Places to Eat!

Applebee's
Food: American
4505 Devine St.
(803) 787-4687
www.applebees.com
Price: $15 and under
Hours: Monday–Thursday
11 a.m.–11:30 p.m., Friday–
Saturday 11 a.m.–12 a.m.,
Sunday 11 a.m.–10 p.m.

Beezer's
Food: American
919 Sumter St.
(803) 771-7771
Price: $6 and under
Hours: Monday–Thursday
11 a.m.–3 a.m., Friday–
Saturday 11 a.m.–4 a.m.,
Sunday 11 a.m.–12 p.m.

Ben and Jerry's
Food: Ice cream
2901 Devine St.
(803) 931-8788

(Ben and Jerry's, continued)
Price: $5 and under
Hours: Monday–Thursday
11 a.m.–10 p.m., Friday–
Saturday 11 a.m.–11 p.m.,
Sunday 2 p.m.–10 p.m.

Carolina Bagel
Food: Breakfast
925 Sumter St.
(803) 799-6676
Price: $7 and under
Hours: Monday–Friday
7 a.m.–6 p.m.,
Saturday 8 a.m.–3 p.m.

Carrabba's
Food: Italian
370 Columbiana Dr.
(803) 407-1811
www.carrabas.com
Price: $20 and under
Hours: Monday–Thursday
4 p.m.–10 p.m.,
Friday 4 p.m.–11 p.m.,
Saturday 3 p.m.–11 p.m.,
Sunday 3 p.m.–10 p.m.

Groucho's Deli
Food: American deli
611 Harden St.
(803) 799-5708
www.grouchos.com
Price: $8 and under
Hours: Monday–Saturday
11 a.m.–4 p.m.

IHOP
Food: American
1031 Assembly St.
(803) 765-0305
www.ihop.com
Price: $7 and under
Hours: Daily 24 hours

Mangia Mangia
Food: Italian
100 State St.
(803) 791-3443
Price: $25 and under
Hours: Monday–Friday
5 p.m.–10 p.m., Saturday–
Sunday 5 p.m.–11 p.m.

Miyo's
Food: Chinese
3250 Forrest Dr.
(803) 743-9996
Price: $12 and under
Hours: Monday–Saturday
10:30 a.m.–2 p.m.,
5:30 p.m.–10 p.m.,
Sunday 11:30 a.m.–2:30 p.m.,
5 p.m.–9:30 p.m.

Monterrey
Food: Mexican
114 Afton Ct.
(803) 749-5928
Price: $6 and under
Hours: Monday–Saturday
11 a.m.–10 p.m.

The Pita Pit
Food: American
2002 Greene St.
(803) 799-4557
www.pitapit.com
Price: $8 and under
Hours: Monday–Saturday
11 a.m.–3 a.m.,
Sunday 12 p.m.–3 a.m.

Ruby Tuesday
Food: American
4600 Devine St.
(803) 790-8974
www.rubytuesday.com
Price: $9 and under
Hours: Monday–Thursday
11 a.m.–10:30 p.m., Friday–
Saturday 11 a.m.–11:30 p.m.,
Sunday 11 a.m.–9:30 p.m.

The Salty Nut
Food: American
2000 Greene St.
(803) 256-4611
www.saltynut.com
Price: $9 and under
Hours: Daily 11 a.m.–12 a.m.

Sammi's Deli
Food: American
919 Sumter St.
(803) 771-7958
Price: $7 and under
Hours: Monday–Thursday
10:30 a.m.–11 p.m., Friday–
Saturday 10:30 a.m.–12 p.m.,
Sunday 11 a.m.–11 p.m.

Sandy's Famous Hot Dogs
Food: American
825 Main St.
(803) 254-6914
Price: $6 and under
Hours: Daily 11 a.m.–10 p.m.

The Village Idiot Pizza & Pub
Food: Pizza
2009 Devine St.
(803) 252-8646
Price: $7 and under
Hours: Daily 11 a.m.–3 a.m.

Yesterday's
Food: American
2030 Devine St.
(803) 799-0196
www.yesterdayssc.com
Price: $8 and under
Hours: Sunday–Wednesday
11:30 a.m.–12 a.m., Thursday–
Saturday 11:30 a.m.–1 a.m.

Other Places to Check Out:
Cool Beans
Garret's
Harper's
Immaculate Consumption
Jungle Jim's
Leo's Wings
Nonnah's
Sharky's

Student Favorites:
Beezer's
Sammi's Deli
The Pita Pit
Groucho's Deli
The Salty Nut
Monterrey's

Grocery Stores:
Bi-Lo
4464 Devine St., Columbia
(803) 738-1108

Kroger
3403 Forrest Dr., Forrest Acres
(803) 738-0225

Piggly Wiggly
3818 Devine St., Columbia
(803) 256-3433

Publix
2800 Rosewood Dr., Columbia
(803) 806-8839

24-Hour Dining:
IHOP

Best Breakfast:
Carolina Bagel

Best Chinese:
Miyo's

Best Pizza:
The Village Idiot Pizza & Pub

Best Wings:
The Salty Nut

Best Healthy:
The Pita Pit

Best Place to Take Your Parents:
Carrabba's

Did You Know?

The **Beezer's delivery guy is well known** on campus for his orangish-red hair and the moped he drives when making deliveries.

Students Speak Out On...
Off-Campus Dining

> **"The Pita Pit, Groucho's, Harper's, and many more restaurants have excellent food with varying price ranges."**

Q "Whatever you can't get on campus you can probably get within walking distance of campus. Being an urban University, we are right downtown and only a few blocks from Five Points, the main downtown shopping area. A few blocks in the other direction is the state capitol. We have whatever you desire, from **excellent vegetarian to Italian, Indian, Japanese, or Middle-Eastern cuisine—** you won't starve!"

Q "I think you could go to a new place every night for a year in the city, but I enjoy are the coffee houses and such. There are so many options it is hard for me to explain. There's **everything from Applebee's to coffee houses to fancy restaurants**. My favorite Italian place is called Mangia Mangia, but Carrabas is good, too. There are a lot of restaurants here, and you would get paid really well if you worked here. My friend works at a Mexican place here, and she is making a bundle!"

Q "The restaurants are really, really good. A common sub place with good prices and awesome food is called Beezer's. Right next to it is a good Greek place called Sammi's Deli. Salty Nut is a great place, too. If you're into **trendy little coffee houses**, there's Cool Beans and Immaculate Consumption."

Q "The hot spot off of campus is definitely Monterrey's; it's **great Mexican food, and it's cheap**!"

Q "Off-campus food is great! We have all the normal pizza places, a sub place called Beezer's, and a pita shop called Pita Pit. There is a **Ben and Jerry's ice cream** parlor, plus about 50 other spots. Food is definitely better off campus."

Q "There's Yesterday's, which is just a little pub-type place, and there's the Village Idiot, a pizza place. There are other restaurants around, like Applebee's and Ruby Tuesday, but **I don't know about much else because I don't get off campus very much**."

Q "If you come to USC, the first thing you will notice is that we are an eating-out town. The **main area for college students is Five Points**, which is right behind campus. This is where the best bars, clubs, and restaurants are. The big USC hangouts are Sharky's, Jungle's, Groucho's, and Garret's."

Q "One thing good about the campus is that it is within walking distance to Five Points. Some of my favorite restaurants are Pita Pit, Salty Nut, Groucho's, and Sandy's. Five Points is also accepting our meal plans this year. For more information, **go to www.5pointsmealplan.com**."

Q "If you want to stay fairly cheap, places like Ruby Tuesday and Applebee's are good places. There is also Leo's Wings right near campus that is reasonably priced, for the hot wing lover like myself. If you want to **go more classy, there is a place called Nonnah's**, which I would only recommend for dessert and coffee. The entrees aren't very large and are high in price."

The College Prowler Take On...
Off-Campus Dining

While students may complain about campus food, the plethora of off-campus restaurants makes up for what may be lacking on campus. Most of the student favorites, such as Five Points, Beezer's, the Salty Nut, and the Pita Pit, are all within walking distance of campus. The diversity of the food choices off campus allows students to choose from virtually any type of ethnic food at a range of prices. And with Columbia being a college town, many restaurants offer late-night deliveries when most other places are closed and it's too late to be walking around campus.

Whatever the occasion, whether it's dinner with friends, a hot date, a late-night study snack, or just an escape from campus food, the off-campus dining scene provides quality food with a broad range of choices for students to enjoy. You will definitely not go hungry in a city like Columbia!

The College Prowler® Grade on
Off-Campus Dining: A-

A high Off-Campus Dining grade implies that off-campus restaurants are affordable, accessible, and worth visiting. Other factors include the variety of cuisine and the availability of alternative options (vegetarian, vegan, Kosher, etc.).

Campus Housing

The Lowdown On...
Campus Housing

Undergrads Living on Campus:
40%

Number of Residence Halls:
23

Best Dorms:
Capstone
Columbia Hall
Horseshoe Apartments

Worst Dorms:
The Towers

Residence Halls:

Bates House

Floors: 9

Total Occupancy: 500

Bathrooms: Community

Coed: Yes, by floor

Residents: Freshmen

Room Types: Traditional

Special Features: Houses the Bates Engineering Community, rooms have a MicroFridge and carpeting, house has a cafeteria, a 24-hour computer lab, a student parking lot

Visitation: 10 a.m.–2 a.m.

Bates West

Floors: 14

Total Occupancy: 400

Bathrooms: Four students share an in-room bathroom

Coed: Yes

Residents: Upperclassmen

Room Types: Apartment

Special Features: Carpeting, refrigerators, adjacent parking, in-hall cafeteria, electronic building access, classroom, TV area, meeting room, pool table, Ping-Pong table, vending machines

Visitation: Self-regulated

Capstone House

Floors: 18

Total Occupancy: 564

Bathrooms: Two double rooms share an adjoining bathroom

(Capstone House, continued)

Coed: Yes

Residents: Mostly upperclassmen

Room Types: Suite

Special Features: Student parking, in-hall cafeteria

Visitation: Monday–Thursday 10 a.m.–2 a.m., Friday–Sunday 12 p.m.–2 a.m.

Columbia Hall *near Moore Busin. School*

Floors: 11

Total Occupancy: 480

Bathrooms: Two double rooms share an adjoining bathroom

Coed: Yes

Residents: All students

Room Types: Suite

Special Features: Houses two substance-free floors, exercise center located in the basement, 24-hour computer lab, carpeted rooms

Visitation: Self-regulated

DeSaussure College

Floors: 3

Total Occupancy: 44

Bathrooms: Four students share an in-room bathroom

Coed: Yes

Residents: Upperclassmen

Room Types: Mostly four-bedroom apartments

Special Features: Carpeting and refrigerator in each apartment, located on the Horseshoe

Visitation: Self-regulated

Douglas (Towers)

Floors: 7

Total Occupancy: 240

Bathrooms: Community

Coed: No, men only

Residents: Freshmen

Room Types: Traditional

Special Features: Academic Center for Excellence on the main floor, MicroFridge in each room, 24-hour computer lab, electronic building access

Visitation: Restricted to main lobby on first floor, floors 2–7 10 a.m.–2 a.m.

Harper/Elliott Colleges

Floors: 3

Total Occupancy: 60

Bathrooms: 2–4 students per bathroom

Coed: Yes

Residents: Upperclassmen

Room Types: Two- and four-bedroom apartments

Special Features: Carpeting and refrigerator in each apartment

Visitation: Self-regulated

Henderson (820)

Floors: 3

Total Occupancy: 24

Bathrooms: Four students per bathroom

Coed: Yes

Residents: Upperclassmen

Room Types: Mostly two-bedroom apartments

(Henderson (820), continued)

Special Features: Includes own kitchen, dining, and living area

Visitation: Self-regulated

Laborde (Towers)

Floors: 7

Total Occupancy: 240

Bathrooms: Community

Coed: Yes, by floor

Residents: Freshmen

Room Types: Traditional

Special Features: Academic Center for Excellence located on first floor, MicroFridge in each room, 24-hour computer lab, vending machines, ice machine, classroom, electronic building access

Visitation: 10 a.m.–2 a.m.

Maxcy College

Floors: 4

Total Occupancy: 182

Bathrooms: Two double rooms share an adjoining bathroom

Coed: Yes

Residents: All freshmen

Room Types: Suite

Special Features: Seminar room, freshmen honors housing, kitchen, social room, and laundry located in basement, electronic building access

Visitation: 10 a.m.–2 a.m.

McBryde Quad

Floors: 3

Total Occupancy: 350

uck hall rooms big

(McBryde Quad, continued)

Bathrooms: Community
Coed: No, men only
Residents: Mostly freshmen
Room Types: Traditional
Special Features: Large social space, mostly Greek residents
Visitation: 10 a.m.–2 a.m.

McClintock

Floors: 3
Total Occupancy: 142
Bathrooms: Community
Coed: No, women only
Residents: Freshmen
Room Types: Traditional
Special Features: Laundry room, carpeting in room
Visitation: 10 a.m.–2 a.m.

Moore (Towers)

Floors: 7
Total Occupancy: 240
Bathrooms: Community
Coed: Yes, by floor
Residents: Freshmen
Room Types: Traditional
Special Features: Wellness and Teaching Fellows Community, 24-hour computer lab, electronic building access
Visitation: 10 a.m.–2 a.m.

Patterson Hall

all girl just renovated

Floors: 9
Total Occupancy: 615
Bathrooms: Community

(Patterson Hall, continued)

Coed: No, women only
Residents: Freshmen
Room Types: Traditional
Special Features: Largest campus residence hall, in-hall cafeteria, double and triple rooms, kitchens on every floor, 24-hour computer lab, carpeting in rooms
Visitation 10 a.m.–2 p.m.

Preston College

– M–F dining hall dine

Floors: 3
Total Occupancy: 240
Bathrooms: Two double rooms share an adjoining bathroom
Coed: Yes
Residents: Sophomores and some freshmen
Room Types: Suite
Special Features: Seminar room, two common rooms, residents required to eat four evening meals per week at in-hall cafeteria (30 faculty dine with the students)
Visitation: Self-regulated

Roost Hall

Floors: 3
Total Occupancy: 230
Bathrooms: Four students share a bathroom
Coed: Yes
Residents: Upperclassmen
Room Types: Two-bedroom apartments

(Roost Hall, continued)

Special Features: Adjacent parking, nearby athletic fields, laundry room, in-hall cafeteria, MicroFridge and carpeting in room

Visitation: Monday–Thursday 10 a.m.–2 a.m.

Sims Hall

Floors: 3

Total Occupancy: 285

Bathrooms: Two double rooms share an adjoining bathroom

Coed: No, women only

Residents: Upperclassmen

Room Types: Suite and five apartment-style rooms

Special Features: Lounge with TV and piano, classroom, laundry, carpeting in room

Visitation: Monday–Thursday 10 a.m.–2 a.m.

Snowden (Towers)

Floors: 7

Total Occupancy: 240

Bathrooms: Community

Coed: No, men only

Residents: All freshmen

Room Types: Traditional

Special Features: Academic Center for Excellence located on main floor, MicroFridge in each room, 24-hour computer lab, electronic building access

Visitation: 10 a.m.–2 a.m.

South Quadrangle

Floors: 4

Total Occupancy: 400

Bathrooms: Private

Coed: Yes

Residents: Upperclassmen

Room Types: Four-bedroom apartments

Special Features: Meeting room, vending machine, multipurpose room, laundry room, electronic building access, refrigerator and carpeting in each apartment

Visitation: Self-regulated

South Tower

Floors: 18

Total Occupancy: 391

Bathrooms: Hall/community bathrooms, 23 women share a bathroom

Coed: No, women only

Residents: Upperclassmen

Room Types: Traditional

Special Features: Mostly Greek, sorority lounges and kitchens on each floor, conference room, lounge, laundry room, electronic building access

Visitation: Monday–Thursday 10 a.m.–2 a.m., Friday–Sunday 12 p.m– 2 a.m.

Thornwell College

Floors: 3

Total Occupancy: 145

Bathrooms: Private

Coed: Yes

(Thornwell College, continued)

Residents: Upperclassmen

Room Types: Two- to four-bedroom apartments

Special Features: Carpeting and refrigerator in room

Visitation: Self-regulated

Wade Hampton Hall

Floors: 4

Total Occupancy: 178

Bathrooms: Community

Coed: No, women only

Residents: Freshmen

Room Types: Traditional

Special Features: TV lounge, study room, laundry room, electronic building access

Visitation: 10 a.m.–2 a.m. No visitation in basement

Woodrow College

Floors: 3

Total Occupancy: 120

Bathrooms: One bathroom in each apartment

Coed: Yes

Residents: Upperclassmen

Room Types: Two- and three-bedroom apartments

Special Features: Carpeting and refrigerator in room

Visitation: Self-regulated

Did You Know?

Students living on campus have **access to free cable and Internet services**.

Special-interest housing includes Maxcy Honors Hall, Bates Engineering Community, Moore's Wellness Community, and Moore's Premedical Community.

Room **inspections take place periodically** to ensure that students are meeting campus regulations.

Room Types:

Traditional – Community bathrooms and two students to a room

Suite-style – Semi-private bathroom adjoins two rooms, two students to a room

Apartment – Two, three, or four students share a common living area, kitchen, and bathroom

Bed Type

Twin extra-long

Available for Rent

MicroFridges

Cleaning Service?

Cleaning services provided for all hall and community bathrooms

What You Get

Air-conditioning, voice, cable and data connections, twin bed, dresser, desk, chair, closet

Also Available

Special-interest housing, wellness housing, no-visitation housing, quiet floors in certain dorms

Students Speak Out On...
Campus Housing

> **"Most of the dorms are okay. You'll have plenty of space. I would live on campus for freshman year, but then I recommend moving off campus sophomore or junior year for more freedom."**

Q "I love Bates West because it is apartment-style. We have **our own bathrooms and kitchens**, and a lot more privacy. I lived in the Towers my first year, and I loved it because of all the people that I got to meet. There was always something going on or someone always knew something to do. It is almost in the center of campus, so you can get to anything within a five-minute walk. My friend stayed in Patterson. She loved it, but I hated it because unlike where I stayed, it was not coed, so if you wanted to have someone spend the night, you couldn't."

Q "I would advise against Bates (freshmen only), Bates West, and the Roost (both upperclassmen). I don't recommend them—not because they are bad, but because unless you have a car and unless you want to take the shuttles all of the time, it is a long walk. These dorms are also far away from Five Points, and **shuttles don't run past 5:30 p.m.**"

Q "The nicest **freshman dorms for girls are Patterson and Bates**. The only negative thing about Bates is that it is very far from the campus. It is a little newer, but it's not as easy to get to and from places from Bates. Patterson is where I stayed my freshman year; it's nice. It is in the center of the campus, so it is very easy to get to and from things. It was close to all my classes, had two parking garages near it, which is very rare, and it was close to many of the main dining facilities."

Q "I'd recommend either Patterson Hall, McClintock, or Wade Hampton. If you happen to be a freshman girl, you will definitely want to try and get Patterson. This is where you will meet the most friendly girls. Stay away from the Towers. McClintock and Wade Hampton are also for freshman girls, but they aren't as large as Patterson. Patterson also has a place to eat downstairs. When you become an upperclassman, I'd recommend East Quad, South Quad, or anything on **the Horseshoe—it's probably the prettiest place on campus**."

Q "The girls' dorms are far better than the guys'. As a girl, I would say to stay at either Patterson or Wade Hampton. **The dorm to stay away from is Bates** because it is on the other end of campus. It isn't bad, but I wouldn't want to stay there. Also, Moore is a coed dorm, and that is the one I stayed in my freshman year. It isn't bad, but it isn't great. I would say stay in Patterson or Wade Hampton, then Moore and Bates if that is the last choice."

Q "I hated Patterson—it has nine floors, and the fire alarms and laundry facilities are awful. But, other than that, it's not too bad. It has a dining area in the basement, and it is easy to meet a lot of different people since it's so big. The Towers are coed, and those are the less strict ones, but they aren't as nice. **Wade Hampton and McClintock aren't too bad**, but they are kind of strict and stuck up."

Q "You get what you pay for. You could pay for an elegant room in the South or East Quad and live like a queen, or you could opt to live in one of the Towers buildings and gag whenever someone uses the restroom in the large communal bathroom and shower area, but you'd save money. If you want to strike a nice balance, the dorm rooms in Capstone aren't all that bad, really. They're not huge, but they're not microscopic. There is **enough space so you're not in your roommate's face, and there is decent closet space**. If you want to strike a balance, I'd go there."

The College Prowler Take On...
Campus Housing

There are advantages and disadvantages to living on campus. Most students find that living on campus freshman year allows them the opportunity to interact with students more and get involved in activities without having to worry about commuting. The quality of the dorm depends on what dorm you choose and your own personal preferences. They come furnished with the bare essentials. The rest is up to him or her. There are coed and single sex dorms for freshmen and dorms with hall or suite-style bathrooms. Some say sharing a community bathroom helps students bond, while others wouldn't dare use a community bathroom without being armed with a can of Lysol.

Visitation policies in some dorms can be a hindrance since most don't allow it late at night, or at least they restrict with members of the opposite sex. There are mandatory hall meetings, rules about quiet hours, and the occasional RA from hell. Students generally rate the dorms average or a bit less than average in terms of cleanliness and quality. It seems as though Patterson and Capstone are the favorites for freshmen, but students admit that even these dorms aren't all that great. On the flip side, if you live on campus, students have the convenience of being able to roll out of bed 15 minutes before class and still make it on time. You've also got the convenience of being surrounded by hundreds of students in the same boat as you, which can sometimes make the transition a whole lot easier.

B-

The College Prowler® Grade on
Campus Housing: B-

A high Campus Housing grade indicates that dorms are clean, well-maintained, and spacious. Other determining factors include variety of dorms, proximity to classes, and social atmosphere.

Off-Campus Housing

The Lowdown On...
Off-Campus Housing

Undergrads in Off-Campus Housing:
60%

Average Rent For:
Studio Apt.: $520/month
1BR Apt.: $670/month
2BR Apt.: $750/month

Popular Areas:
Atrium Place
Sterling
University Commons
Whaley's Mill

For Assistance Contact:
Off-Campus Housing Dept.
(803) 777-3196
www.sa.sc.edu/rhuu/ ochsproplisting.htm

Students Speak Out On...
Off-Campus Housing

 "Living off campus can be really convenient. It's definitely cheaper than living on campus."

Q "I live off campus, and it's great. I live in an apartment with other college students who go to South Carolina. It is really fun. I lived in a dorm my freshman year, and that was fun. It was good for one year, but I didn't want to do it again. I would, however, say to **live in a dorm freshman year because you will meet a lot of people** in your hall who will become your friends, and that is always good if you don't know anyone here."

Q "I have lived off campus for two of my three years here, and off-campus convenience depends on where you live. One year, I was literally on campus in a house that was closer to my classes than any dorm—this is pricey, however. **Columbia is incredibly reasonable** as far as cost of living goes (which is good for poor students working their way through college). You can easily live off campus with a roommate or two for less than it costs to live on campus."

Q "Off-campus housing is **not very convenient if you don't have a car**."

Q "There are a lot of apartments, but it's really hard to actually get a good one, especially for freshmen. There is University Commons, which is pretty nice, but it's pretty far from campus. You would definitely have to drive to class, but it is a pain because parking is so hard. **I would recommend living in the dorms**."

Q "Freshmen are required to live on campus their first year unless they have family within 50 miles. I live off campus now and have done so since second semester. Off-campus living is nice, but at times, **you miss out on some of the things that are happening on campus.**"

Q "The University of South Carolina is an urban campus, but it all **depends how much you want to spend**. Usually, it will cost about 300–500 dollars a month for a decent place."

Q "Off-campus housing is great. There are many apartments, and there are two huge neighborhoods known as Shannon and Rosewood. These **neighborhoods are all pretty much run by college students.**"

Q "I lived at the University Commons for the last three years since I **wasn't a big fan of sharing a small dorm room** with someone else. I personally think that I needed the freshman experience of living on campus, but after one year, I decided that I had enough."

Q "I'm not sure about the convenience of living off campus; I'm going to be a sophomore next year. However, the **traffic and parking present great problems** from what I hear."

Q "There are many places to stay that are close to campus, but you have to **find one that has a lease available**, which is hard to come by. But if you get a garage space and live away, I think you will be okay."

Q "On-campus housing is very convenient, and I would have to say that it is worth it for at least another year. About your junior year, the **rules and regulations of dorm life can get weary.**"

The College Prowler Take On...
Off-Campus Housing

Many students come to prefer off-campus housing at some point in their college career. Whether it's because of the greater freedom, the price, or just because they're ready for a new phase in their lives, some prefer off-campus housing in spite of the distance from campus. The school-sponsored complex, University Commons, is where many students choose, even though there are some closer ones. The price depends on the location, size, and quality of the apartment—off-campus housing is not always cheaper than on campus. The price of gas and a reserved garage space are also a factor, since both are necessary for anyone who commutes. Other additional costs include the cost of furniture, utilities, and groceries.

The main problem with living off campus is that students often feel secluded from the action. The convenience of the campus activities right outside your door is gone, you can no longer trek to the library any time you need to, or even walk to the Russell House for a late-night meal with friends. It is all a question of whether your priority is freedom or convenience—a choice between freedom with added responsibility or convenience with less flexibility. However, the option of quality off-campus housing is definitely there for those who decide to go that route.

B+

The College Prowler® Grade on
Off-Campus
Housing: B+

A high grade in Off-Campus Housing indicates that apartments are of high quality, close to campus, affordable, and easy to secure.

Diversity

The Lowdown On...
Diversity

African American:
12%

Native American:
Less than 1%

Asian American:
3%

White:
72%

Hispanic:
2%

Unknown:
9%

International:
1%

Out-of-State:
24%

Political Activity

USC is located in a very conservative area of the country, but students of all political opinions find ways to express their views. Politically-involved students really have the chance to make an impact, especially because USC is in the middle of South Carolina's capital and only a few blocks away from the state house. Protests are pretty frequent, and groups often host political debates on campus in an attempt to get even more students interested in the legislative action taking place.

Gay Pride

Anti-gay sentiments are not expressed visibly at USC, but this may be in part because the gay population remains relatively quiet.

Economic Status

The majority of USC students are middle- to upper-class in terms economic status. You will see a few cruising around in a new Mercedes their parents bought them, but for the most part, the students are not incredibly wealthy.

Minority Clubs

There is a total of 13 minority clubs on campus, but they are generally unseen and unheard. The African American groups are the most well-recognized minority organizations on campus, and there are a few African American fraternities and sororities.

Most Popular Religion

Christianity is by far the most prominent religion on campus. There are a lot of religious clubs and organizations, most of which are Christian-oriented, but there are also organizations for students of other religious convictions.

Students Speak Out On...
Diversity

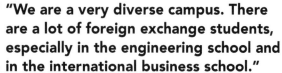

"We are a very diverse campus. There are a lot of foreign exchange students, especially in the engineering school and in the international business school."

Q "I don't know about specifics, but **different groups are represented on campus** through things like the Association of African American Students, Brothers of Nubian Decent, Filipino Association, Bisexual Gay Lesbian Association, and a lot more."

Q "I feel that our campus is very diverse, but we **still have a long way to go**."

Q "Since USC has a **great international program**, you see students from all kinds of backgrounds every day. There are even international dorms and meeting houses."

Q "The campus is not as diverse as most places, I would expect, but **there are no problems**."

Q "The campus is pretty diverse. There are **different racial and religious groups** all over the campus. Everyone celebrates in their own way, and that hasn't caused a problem for anyone."

Q "USC has a pretty diverse student body. I don't know the exact statistics, but you can find different kinds of people all over campus, and **they all seem to have an organization**."

Q "The campus is pretty diverse. There are a lot of South Carolinians, but a lot of **people come from all over the country and other countries**. I don't know anyone from another country, but some of the sports teams have international students."

Q "USC is not very diverse. Many people are **still stuck in a narrow-minded perspective**. Even though USC is located in Columbia, there are still many people who live out in the country, isolated from people and retaining the ideals of their parents and grandparents. And we all know how times change."

Q "I think that **USC is quite diverse**. The campus definitely has its cultured sides to it. Students come from all over the nation and world to attend USC. I can honestly say that in every class I had each semester, there were always a few international students along with a large group of out-of-state students."

Q "**USC is really diverse**. There are lots of international students."

Q "Carolina is diverse. **There is something for everyone**, no matter what you are involved in, and if there isn't, you can easily start the organization. Many people from all over the country, and even the world, come to Carolina to go to school."

The College Prowler Take On...
Diversity

While many USC students claim that the campus is very diverse, the statistics indicate otherwise. The campus is 79 percent Caucasian and 15 percent African American, leaving only six percent for other nationalities. One reason that students may be under the impression that the campus is more diverse than it is in reality, is that there are many organizations that cater to individual ethnic groups, such as the Filipino American Student Association, the Hindu Students Council, and the Students Association for Latin America that increase students' awareness of ethnic groups on campus. And the truth of the matter is, that many students do not come from an incredibly diverse background, so the presence of a small number of international students or persons of a different ethnic background makes the campus diverse to them.

While USC is certainly not among the most diverse schools in the nation, it is actually pretty consistent with the amount of diversity found at other universities across the nation. In general, colleges across the nation are not incredibly diverse. But USC has a long way to go before it may be considered truly diverse.

The College Prowler® Grade on
Diversity: C

A high grade in Diversity indicates that ethnic minorities and international students have a notable presence on campus and that students of different economic backgrounds, religious beliefs, and sexual preferences are well-represented.

Guys & Girls

The Lowdown On...
Guys & Girls

Male Undergrads:
45%

Female Undergrads:
55%

Birth Control Available?

Yes, free condoms are available to students. At the Women's Care Clinic, students can also purchase birth control pills, Depo-Provera injections, Lunelle monthly injections, vaginal contraceptive rings, the Ortho Evra contraceptive skin patch, and diaphragms.

Hookups or Relationships?

The odds of finding a significant other at USC are really good, just because there are so many options. There are slightly more females than males on campus, but you wouldn't even be able to tell by walking around campus. While many students date or hook up, the majority of students are not involved in serious, long-term relationships.

Best Place to Meet Guys/Girls

Where's the best place to get your flirt on? The most obvious place would be at one of the many bars in the area or at a house party, where students go to relax and have fun. It's also not too uncommon to meet an attractive guy or girl in class or just around campus, while you're grabbing a bite to eat at the Russell House. And you will definitely find some beautiful people at the grassy Horseshoe area in the middle of campus, especially when it starts to get warm and guys and girls don their bathing suits and lay out to work on their tans.

Social Scene

The social scene at USC is always bustling. Because the campus is so big, and because there is such a big student body population, the parties are plentiful. Students generally enjoy taking the opportunity to get away from their studies. On the contrary, not everyone at Carolina is a social butterfly. You will find different kinds of people, some who don't care to socialize at all, and others who can't seem to stop. However, students in general are quite amiable, and it's not hard to find friends, whether it's in class, at the dorms, or out and about around campus. The abundance of social activity at USC is one of the things that make it such an exciting place to live and learn.

Did You Know?

Top Places to Find Hotties:
1. Frat parties
2. The Horseshoe
3. Five Points or the Vista

Top Places to Hook Up:
1. Frat parties
2. Dorm rooms
3. The Horseshoe
4. House parties
5. Clubs

Dress Code

At USC, pretty much anything goes in terms of clothing. Most people tend to dress casually in whatever keeps them cool and comfortable. Some students don't even bother getting out of their pajamas before going to class. But there are also some people who don't go out in public without wearing a dress or a tie. Punky, preppy, messy, artsy—whatever your style, you will undoubtedly find your niche here at USC. Even though shorts or jeans and T-shirts are the norm, clothing generally doesn't attract too much attention, even if someone is wearing something completely out of the ordinary.

Students Speak Out On...
Guys & Girls

"I believe that we have some pretty unbelievably hot girls at USC, and I will say the guys aren't bad either because of me!"

 "Guys are really Southern and have a great deal of Southern pride, especially the fraternity guys. They all wear Rainbow flip-flops, croakies, short khaki shorts, and shaggy haircuts. **It all depends on your taste** in guys, I guess."

"The guys from up north are rude. The **guys from the South are usually pretty generous and courteous**. The girls from up north are usually pretty nice, but they can also be kind of rude. Girls from the South are nice and sweet. I'd say there are attractive guys on campus. The girls on campus are attractive as well."

"Yeah the **girls are hot**! As for the guys, I don't want to judge, but yeah, we are hot, too."

"Like anywhere, **there are good-looking ones and not-so-good-looking ones**. If you aren't used to the Southern way, like I wasn't at first, the southerners will seem a little weird—you have to get used to them. But overall, campus has a variety of people. I am positive you will find a place to belong."

"There are definitely a lot of hot guys (if you like southern boys) and most of the girls look alike (blonde, Southern girls). If you look a little different, I think the guys take it as a plus. **The guys are outnumbered by the girls**, though, so that sucks."

Q "As far as the girls go, there's a lot of eye candy. If you're into girls, there's a whole lot of them. There's a **big stigma here against homosexuals**, though, except in three cities: Columbia, Greenville, and Charleston. They are like the oasis spots in a region filled with prejudice. Also, if you are for gay rights, there's a group here called the GBLA (Gay Bisexual and Lesbian Association). It's a student group that advocates for equal treatment. They're actually getting a pretty big following at USC."

Q "I have traveled through 45 of the 50 states, and I have **never been anywhere with as many hot girls**. I would assume there would be some reciprocity when it comes to guys."

Q "There aren't any hot guys, really—sorry. I don't know why, but **Columbia is severely lacking in hot men**."

Q "I'd say there is a wide variety of people when it comes to appearances. There is a large population of good-looking guys on campus. **Dating material? I'm not so sure about that one**."

Q "I think midway through freshman year, **all guys tend to look alike**. You have the typical frat boys, a few skaters, and an occasional goth. But they are just your average-looking guys, nothing too special, nothing too weird. The same goes for the girls. I think you can put just about every girl in a category: your sorority girls, your sporty girls, the girls that look like they are constantly just getting out of bed—nothing too spectacular. You do find your occasional hot guy (speaking from my female point of view), but I would not say that USC is known for its good-looking guys."

The College Prowler Take On...
Guys & Girls

It's true that down here in South Carolina the weather is sweltering, but the guys and girls are even hotter! According to students, the guys tend to be more chivalrous and charming than the average, and the girls are beautiful, even if many of them may fall into the typical Southern belle category. They are the blonde and the beautiful, and the package generally comes with a distinctive Southern drawl, and of course, that perfect golden-brown tan from hours out in the hot Carolina sun.

This is not to say that all girls and guys are good-looking. It just depends on what you find attractive. There are many different kinds of people with varying appearances. There are those who dress up in skirts and suits every day and those who go to class in their pajamas. There are also the goths, the skaters, the Greeks, the athletes, and the intellectuals. It really just boils down to a matter of personal preference. Based on the universally-accepted attractive characteristics, students seem think that USC is rather well-endowed with beautiful people.

The College Prowler® Grade on
Guys: B

A high grade for Guys indicates that the male population on campus is attractive, smart, friendly, and engaging, and that the school has a decent ratio of guys to girls.

The College Prowler® Grade on
Girls: A

A high grade for Girls not only implies that the women on campus are attractive, smart, friendly, and engaging, but also that there is a fair ratio of girls to guys.

Athletics

The Lowdown On...
Athletics

Athletic Division:
Division I

Conference:
Southeastern (SEC)

School Mascot:
The Gamecock

**Men Playing
Varsity Sports:**
285 (4%)

**Women Playing
Varsity Sports:**
183 (2%)

Men's Varsity Sports:

Baseball
Basketball
Football
Golf
Soccer
Swimming
Tennis
Track and field
(indoor and outdoor)

Women's Varsity Sports:

Basketball
Cross country
Golf
Soccer
Softball
Swimming
Tennis
Track and field
(indoor and outdoor)
Volleyball

Club Sports:

Bowling
Frisbee (women's)
Karate (women's)
Lacrosse
Martial arts
Racquetball (men's)
Rugby (women's)
Sailing
Scuba (women's)
Soccer (men's)
Volleyball (women's)
Water skiing
Weight lifting

Intramurals:

Basketball
Bowling
Field hockey
Flag football
Frisbee
Golf
Racquetball
Soccer (indoor and outdoor)
Softball
Table tennis
Tennis
Volleyball
Water polo

Athletic Fields

Williams Brice Stadium, fields at the Blatt PE Center

Getting Tickets

Tickets for sporting events are available to students for free at the Russell House and are usually easy to obtain, as long as it's not a huge game. Students usually have to win a drawing in order to get tickets to the USC/Clemson football game because there are not enough tickets to go around.

Most Popular Sports

Football is, by far, the most popular sport. Not necessarily because the team is incredibly great, but because USC has got some diehard football fans. Baseball and basketball also draw pretty big crowds, both with great facilities and good teams.

Best Place to Take a Walk

Finlay Park, the Horseshoe

Gyms/Facilities

Blatt PE Center

Located on Wheat Street, the Blatt offers weight lifting equipment, fitness and aerobics classes, outdoor facilities (football, rugby, soccer, softball, tennis, volleyball), and indoor facilities (badminton, basketball, pool, racquetball, squash, volleyball). Although the facilities at Strom Thurmond Wellness and Fitness Center far surpass those at Blatt, the students still go to Blatt to take advantage of the aerobics and fitness classes offered there.

Strom Thurmond Wellness and Fitness Center

The Strom Thurmond Center is a source of pride for USC, both because of the quality of the newer equipment, and the sheer size of the facility itself. With its convenient location on Assembly Street, most students go to the Strom Thurmond Center rather than the Blatt, even though it might mean fighting a crowd during peak hours of the day when students are more likely to work out.

Students Speak Out On...
Athletics

{ **"Varsity sports are huge here. Our football team is really getting good. IM sports are also big. They have a ton of sports you can play. They are really competitive and also incredibly fun at the same time."**

Q "USC is in the SEC, which is **the biggest sports conference in the nation**. Gamecock football is absolutely huge at USC. We have one of the most dominant sports programs in the country. Intramural (IM) sports are big as well."

Q "One of the greatest highlights of coming to South Carolina is being able to attend varsity sports in arguably the best athletic conference in America. On a weekly basis, I have the **opportunity to see the best athletes in the country**. We have been tremendously successful. You haven't experienced football until you've gone to a SEC football game in the South. It is the most ridiculous fun, even if you aren't a big football fan. All day Saturday is spent dressed up, tailgating, and partying. And this is before we go into our 90,000 capacity stadium for the game, which is almost always televised nationally. And unlike many large universities, all the tickets to every event are free."

Q "Sports are very popular on campus, both IM and varsity. I think that if you like football, you would love our games. There are **80,000 plus people in our stadiums** during the games and over 100,000 people that tailgate. It's a blast, even if you aren't a big football fan. Most of our teams do really, really well! My friend plays IM soccer, and she loves it."

Q "Varsity sports are very big. The football team is especially big. Football games are like one huge party. Before the games, **people will tailgate for hours** and eat and drink. The football games average about 82,000 people per game. Football dominates the varsity sports, but the basketball teams are also very good. IM sports on campus are also pretty good. They have everything—flag football, soccer, softball, basketball, volleyball, tennis, golf, racquetball, ultimate Frisbee, badminton, bowling, floor hockey, and sand volleyball. Last spring, the new PE facility was made available for students, and it is absolutely gorgeous. It has six basketball courts, indoor and outdoor pools, and an indoor rock climbing wall."

Q "Gamecock football is the best experience I have ever had. We have the **best fans in the Southeast**. Even when our team sucked and never won, fans were always there. Now that we are winning again, it's even better!"

Q "Football is huge, of course. Gotta love them Cocks! I only went to football games, but basketball and baseball are big also. **Fraternities and sororities are heavily involved in IM sports**."

Q "The big sport here is football. Everyone loves the Carolina Gamecocks, and you'll rarely see a more animated, fervent bunch of fans anywhere. **Our big rival is the Clemson Tigers**."

Q "**Football season is the theme of the fall**. After that, it dwindles down until next football season. There are lots of IM sports."

Q "Varsity sports aren't a big deal except for basketball—both the men's and women's teams are pretty good and attract decent crowds. **IM sports are really fun** and popular with a lot of people."

Q "Intramurals at USC seem to be pretty common among sororities and fraternities, church organizations, and other extracurricular clubs. **Sports seem to play a large part in these particular organizations**. So if you're interested in intramurals, I recommend you join a club of some sort that would provide an organized team."

Q "Football is a huge sport on campus, and baseball is large also. Many of the other sports have a good following and are great to watch. There are **many opportunities for intramurals on campus**."

The College Prowler Take On...
Athletics

In case you haven't noticed from the student responses, football is pretty much the focus of the sports calendar for USC students. Students really make a big deal out of tailgating and attending the games, even if they just do it for the social aspect rather than actually watching the game. Sports are exciting. The football team has made it to bowl games. And the baseball team is getting better and better each year.

On the other hand, intramural sports experience minimal fan turn out, but are still a fun way for students to get together and have fun. Anyone can join an intramural team, and there are several to choose from (there are actually more intramural sports teams than there are varsity sports teams). Many students create intramural teams through a club or organization, but any individual can sign up to be on a team. Students can choose from sports such as crew, rugby, soccer, tennis, and many more. For more information on USC athletics, you can go to *http://uscsports.collegesports.com*. Whether it's high athletic participation or great school spirit you're looking for, USC athletics have the best of both worlds.

B+

The College Prowler® Grade on
Athletics: B+

A high grade in Athletics indicates that students have school spirit, sports programs are respected, games are well-attended, and intramurals are a prominent part of student life.

Nightlife

The Lowdown On...
Nightlife

Club and Bar Prowler:
Popular Nightlife Spots!

Club Crawler:

There is a wide variety of clubs at USC, ranging in atmosphere, age group, and food selection. These are some of the most popular clubs where students like to party, grab a drink, and relax after a long week.

Banana Joe's Island Party

700 Gervais St.

(803) 806-8250

www.bananajoescolumbia.com

Banana Joe's is one of the few clubs in the area that hosts College Night (on Thursdays) for students 18 and over. Located in the Vista, the club is close to campus and is a favorite among students who want to show off their dance moves, listen to some live music, play pool, or watch TV. The cover charge varies depending on the event.

Jillian's

800 Gervais St.
(803) 779-7789
www.jilliansbilliards.com

Jillian's provides a perfect outlet for the dining sports fan, as well as the college student itching for a night out on the town. It is not as college-oriented as many of the clubs in town. It caters to the interest of crowds ranging from college students to middle-aged adults. Some perks include the 15 television monitors and 13 big-screen televisions, as well as a full dining menu and music from DJs and live bands. You must be 21 to get in after 9 p.m., and there is sometimes a cover for special events.

Liquid Nightlife

812 Harden St.
(803) 765-0405

Liquid Nightlife, located in the Five Points area, is another place where the under-21 crowd can party and dance. The crowd is younger, but there is also the after-work crowd that goes. The atmosphere is always intense and energetic. While there is a cover charge, once you're in, you're set to bump uglies all night long.

Rafter's

638 Harden St.
(803) 256-2741

Rafter's is known for its variety of good music, ranging from country to dance, hard rock, and hip hop. Also located in Five Points, they provide a late-night menu, and for your drinking pleasure, an array of domestic and imported beer, wine, and liquor. The intimate atmosphere, dance floor, pool tables, televisions, and video games have made Rafter's a USC favorite and a 12-time winner of a *Free Times* "Best of" award.

Rio Nightlife

1736 Main St.
(803) 765-0911
www.rionightlife.com

Rio Nightlife's Latin twist is what separates it from the other clubs in the area. They occasionally offer free salsa lessons to the public, and ladies (21 and over) will never pay a cover charge. Tuesday nights are the only nights when the 18-and-up crowd can enter. You must be at least 21 to get in all other nights. Rio Nightlife is a classy place to go for students who want a little dinner, a little dancing, and a little relaxation.

Bar Prowler:

USC students love going to bars, and in Columbia, they certainly have a large selection to choose from. These are some of the area's most popular bars.

The Cock Pit

805 Harden St.

(803) 765-0110

The name itself indicates that The Cock Pit the Gamecocks' stomping ground. It is open until 3 a.m., making it a perfect hangout for zany night owls.

Crocodile Rocks

700A Gervais St.

(803) 252-ROCK

"To duel is cool." Crocodile Rocks' dueling pianos provide versatile entertainment for adults 21 and older. A $5 cover charge gets you in, where you can order from their full menu, get a drink from the bar, and enjoy some of the most bizarre entertainment in town, including the dueling pianos.

Delaney's

741 Saluda Ave.

(803) 779-2345

www.delaneyspub.com

Delaney's has a casual Irish atmosphere and live original and acoustic music, both Irish and American styles. The full-menu pub offers a variety of alcoholic beverages, specialty imported beers, desserts, and

(Delaney's, continued)

specialty coffees. There is no age requirement and no cover charge, making it cheap and easy for college students.

Group Therapy

2107 Greene St.

(803) 256-1203

www.grouptherapybar.com

Enduring the hustle and bustle of Columbia's nightlife for the past 25 years, Group Therapy knows how to please its customers. While this Group Therapy will not relieve you of your traumatic experiences, you can at least drown your sorrows with a glass of imported beer, although you must be at least 21. They have live music on Acoustic Therapy Thursdays and a DJ on Saturdays.

Sharky's at Five Points

636 Harden St.

(803) 779-8337

At Sharky's, you can choose from over 100 kinds of beers or order from their menu. They have appetizers, wings, calzones, hamburgers, and chicken. It's a convenient place for college students to go, especially since there is no cover, and the minimum age is 18. Or, if you don't feel like leaving your dorm, they offer free delivery by calling 256-BUDS. Their specials include $2 Jim Beam, $2 vodka all the time, and free pizza during happy hour Monday–Friday.

Other Places to Check Out:

Art Bar
Dr. Rocco's
The Flip Side
Goatfeathers
Jungle Jim's
The Knock Knock Club
Mallard's Lounge
Momentum
Pavlov's
Publik House
Salty Nut
Yesterday's

Student Favorites:

Banana Joe's Island Party
The Cock Pit
Sharky's at Five Points

Cheapest Place to Get a Drink:

Most of the bars in Five Points and the Vista have competitive prices for drinks, with specials on certain nights.

Primary Areas with Nightlife:

Five Points
The Vista

Bars Close At:

Between 2 and 3 a.m.

Favorite Drinking Games:

A$$hole
Circle of Death
F*#* the dealer

Useful Resources for Nightlife:

www.accesssouthcarolina.com/columbia/sc/nlife.htm

What to Do if You're Not 21

These bars have under-21 nights: Banana Joe's Island Party, Liquid Nightlife, Rio Nightlife, Sharky's at Five Points.

Organization Parties

Many organizations on campus throw good parties, particularly athletic organizations. In most cases, pretty much anyone can go to these by paying a minimal cover for the cost of the alcohol. Depending on the organization, there may or may not be alcohol involved, but either way, organization parties are generally well attended. Several different organizations will have parties on any given weekend, but pretty much the only way to find out about them is by word of mouth.

Frats

See the Greek section!

Students Speak Out On...
Nightlife

> **"There are a couple of clubs you can get into being under 21, but you have to be 21 to get in at most of the bars unless you have a few connections."**

Q "Most of the bars we go to are located in Five Points. There are also some in the Vista, but **they are very strict about underagers** going there, and it's mostly for the older crowd. All the bars are for people who are at least 21 years old, but it is pretty easy to get by with a fake ID in Five Points. The only problem is SLED, the South Carolina Law Enforcement Division. They are pretty rough on underage kids. There are a lot more bars in Columbia than clubs. I basically hang out at the bars. My favorites are Sharky's and the Cock Pit."

Q "We have the hot spot called **Five Points, and it has tons of bars**. There is at least one for each individual out there—gay or straight, preppie or punky. It's so much fun! There is always something going on down there. You have Sharky's, Knock Knock, Group Therapy, Delaney's, and that's just to name a few."

Q "I love Five Points. Some people hate it, but there are like 15 or so bars there, a couple of which are like bar/dance clubs. There is also the Vista, which is springing up now, and a lot of the almost out-of-school/just-graduated crowd goes down there. But, you usually **don't even want to go to the bars during football season** because there is so much going on besides that."

Q "Five Points is great! **Talk about a lot of underage drinking**! You have to be careful of SLED, though. Undercover guys come around every once and a while. Some hot spots are Jungle Jim's, Pavlov's, Sharky's, Village Idiot, and Flip Side; I could go on and on."

Q "Because USC comprises a large part of downtown Columbia, there are plenty of choices for bars. **I do not drink or party because my education is a big thing** to me, and I don't see a point in paying that much money to get drunk. But if that's your thing, I have heard that Banana Joe's, Cock Pit, Rafters, and Momentum are good."

Q "The bar scene is many and varied. My two favorite bars are The Publik House, which is in the style of an **old-fashioned Irish pub**, and Goatfeathers, which is more dark and romantic and a place where a lot of beautiful people hang out."

Q "Bars are really good in Columbia! Dr. Rocco's, Pavlov's, Jungle Jim's, Crocodile Rocks, and Cock Pit are my favorites. There are about 18 bars in Five Points where the young college kids go. The Vista is also about the same distance away, and is where you go when you don't want to be around a whole bunch of drunken college people. Both places are lots of fun. **The bar scene is probably one of the best things about USC**."

Q "At night, the University has a shuttle system that takes students down to Five Points and back to campus—it is really convenient and nice. They have just about any type of bar you would want to be in. The Vista is also close by, and has more clubs and such like Jillian's and Banana Joe's. **It's really a hopping college city when school is in session**."

Q "There aren't too many parties in the sense that one thinks of. It's more like **people get wasted in their dorm rooms** by themselves. The bars are okay and the clubs are decent."

Q "From what I hear, bars in Five Points are a little strict because Columbia **police have been really cracking down on them**."

The College Prowler Take On...
Nightlife

The nightlife in Columbia revolves mainly around Five Points and the Vista, where bars and clubs are abundant and alcohol flows. Drinking is a favorite pastime on weekend nights, which can sometimes be problematic for the under-21 crowd. The busiest night of the week, thirsty Thursdays, sees students flocking to bars or buying kegs for parties. Underage students use fake IDs or scope out places that don't card at all. But they're still at risk of being caught by the South Carolina Law Enforcement Department (SLED) officers, who sometimes go undercover for the specific purpose of finding underage drinkers.

Most of the clubs in Columbia are for the over-21 crowd, but some designate certain nights for those 18 and older. For instance, Banana Joe's Island Party is a club that has College Night on Thursdays, with special contests and activities to entertain college students 18 and older. Columbia nightlife would be better if there were more places that catered to younger students, but there are not many. Students believe that the best part about the nightlife at USC is the numerous bars where they can have a drink. Underage students can participate, and often do, but they have their fun knowing that there is a possibility of getting caught.

A-

The College Prowler® Grade on

Nightlife: A-

A high grade in Nightlife indicates that there are many bars and clubs in the area that are easily accessible and affordable. Other determining factors include the number of options for the under-21 crowd and the prevalence of house parties.

Greek Life

The Lowdown On...
Greek Life

Number of Fraternities:
18

Undergrad Men in Fraternities:
14%

Number of Sororities:
12

Undergrad Women in Sororities:
15%

Fraternities:
Alpha Phi Alpha
Alpha Tau Omega
Chi Psi
Delta Tau Delta
Delta Upsilon
Kappa Alpha Psi
Kappa Alpha Order
Kappa Sigma
Lambda Chi Alpha
Omega Psi Phi
Phi Beta Sigma
Phi Sigma Kappa
Pi Kappa Phi
Sigma Alpha Epsilon
Sigma Chi
Sigma Nu
Sigma Phi Epsilon
Tau Kappa Epsilon

Sororities:
Alpha Chi Omega
Alpha Delta Pi
Alpha Kappa Alpha
Chi Omega
Delta Delta Delta
Delta Gamma
Delta Zeta
Kappa Delta
Kappa Kappa Gamma
Sigma Gamma Rho
Zeta Phi Beta
Zeta Tau Alpha

Other Greek Organizations:
Alpha Phi Omega
Epsilon Sigma Alpha
Fraternity Council
Kappa Kappa Psi
Omega Phi Alpha
Sorority Council
Tau Beta Sigma

Students Speak Out On...
Greek Life

> **"Greek life provides a crucial way to break the studies. The campus is now trying to crack down on Greeks, but Greek organizations provide or fund the vast majority of happenings on this campus."**

Q "I think that the sororities are definitely dominating. They were really bad in my dorm (Patterson), but I don't like sororities. Greek life is pretty big on campus. I was one of the few girls who didn't rush my freshman year, but there are plenty of other things to do. The fraternities aren't too bad, though. There are a lot of cliques, at least in my class, but you can **still have a great social life without joining one**."

Q "I did not join a sorority until I was a sophomore, and I actually had more fun my freshman year, but then again, it was my first year away from home. **Certain bars are Greek-dominated**, and you tend to feel like an outsider if you are not Greek, but it's not like that everywhere. I'd say that about 98 percent of Homecoming is done by Greeks. If you are not Greek, it is not a big deal, but it can help you out a lot, too. If you look under USC's Web page and go to student organizations, you can see some of the chapters."

Q "I wouldn't say that Greek life dominates the school, but if you go Greek, it probably will dominate your life. A few of the **sororities built multi-million dollar Greek houses**, so I would say rush one that has a new house!"

Q "I do not think that Greek life dominates the social scene at all. I am in a Greek service sorority, and I just love it. We aren't the type that goes out and parties all the time, but we are awesome friends, all of us, and we know how to have a good time. **We know the times when we need to do our service work** as well. But anyway, there are a lot of sororities and fraternities if you are interested, but it isn't like you have to be in one to fit in."

Q "Greek life does dominate the social scene, especially your freshman year. I did not go Greek, however, I am very close with a fraternity, and all my friends are in sororities. I still have a blast and don't pay a dime. If you join, **Greek life will run you about $1,000 in dues alone**."

Q "I didn't join a sorority because I already knew a lot of people when I came here**. I suggest rushing, though, to meet people**. If you end up liking a certain fraternity or sorority, then go for it. It really doesn't matter one way or another, though."

Q "Greek life is pretty big here at South Carolina. I am not involved in it because it is not my thing. I have friends that are in it, and they love it. I also have friends that aren't in it, and they like not being involved. If you do it, and it is your thing, **you will meet a lot of friends and have fun**. If you don't, you will still meet a lot of people by going to classes and hanging out downtown."

Q "If you want to make Greek life dominate your social scene, then it's your option. At USC, **everyone has a fair opportunity to get involved** without having to be dedicated to Greek life."

Q "I would say that Greek life has a big part in the social scene. **Most people are a part of Greek life—** Go Tri Delt!"

Q "Greek life here is vibrant, but not dominating. I have a lot of friends in fraternities and sororities, and they enjoy it, but I also have many other friends who are not Greek. I am not in a fraternity, and I do not feel like I am missing out on anything. I have many friends and an active social life. Up until now, there has not been any Greek housing on campus, so Greeks have not been as dominant here as they are some places. They built five Greek houses right on the periphery of campus, which seems to be best for everyone. **They have their life, which seems to be pretty positive**, without infringing on those who maybe have differing values."

Q "It hardly dominates the social scene, but Greek life is definitely noticeable and usually **a positive aspect of campus**."

The College Prowler Take On...
Greek Life

Greeks are the minority at USC, but the people who are involved are very vocal and visible about their organization. So Greek life seems a lot more prominent on campus than it really is. Most students agree that Greek life is a major part of the social scene, but it does not dominate. The completion of Greek housing on campus seems to have increased the number of Greeks on campus. However, even students who are not Greek have the opportunity to meet plenty of friends and get involved in activities that are not Greek-related. If you want Greek life to dominate your social life, it can, but it doesn't have to.

All of the Greek societies sponsor some sort of community service. They also organize formals, participate in intramural sports, and have mixers, where they get together with other societies. The cost of joining a society can be pretty expensive, both monetarily and in terms of time, but most find it to be worth it. There are also the Greek service societies and honor societies, which are less expensive to join, and focus more on academics and community service rather than partying. These societies usually have inductions in the spring because qualification depends on grades from the first semester. Whether it's a social, service, or academic society, Greek life is bustling at USC, and it's constantly expanding and improving.

The College Prowler® Grade on
Greek Life: B+

A high grade in Greek Life indicates that sororities and fraternities are not only present, but also active on campus. Other determining factors include the variety of houses available and the respect the Greek community receives from the rest of the campus.

Drug Scene

The Lowdown On...
Drug Scene

Most Prevalent Drugs on Campus:
Alcohol
Ecstasy
Marijuana

Alcohol-Related Referrals:
357

Alcohol-Related Arrests:
24

Drug-Related Referrals:
100

Drug-Related Arrests:
46

Drug Counseling Programs

Alcohol and Drug Dependency Program
(585) 275-3161

This program treats patients with alcohol and drug problems through therapy and substance abuse sessions.

Counseling and Human Development Center
(585) 777-5223

This health center provides a substance abuse workshop, which increases students' personal awareness of their relationship with drugs, and helps them make healthier lifestyle choices.

Thomson Student Health Center
(585) 275-2361 or (585) 275-3113

This facility helps with smoking cessation programs.

Students Speak Out On...
Drug Scene

"Of course, like any large university, drugs are around if you want them, but I've never seen them pressured on anyone. Pretty much, if you want them you, can get them. But it's possible to stay away from it all."

Q "The **only illegal drug you see on campus is weed**. A lot of people smoke weed; it's not hard to find. There are a lot of other drugs used, but people usually keep it on the DL (down low) and don't really make known what they're doing."

Q "There are a lot of drugs on campus—**a lot of X (ecstasy)** and pot. The pot is all schwag (really bad weed), though."

Q "Honestly, I don't do drugs, and I have **no idea about the drug scene**. I know people do them here just like at every other university around the United States, but that is really all I know about the drug scene."

Q "I have never been offered drugs, but it might be because I don't hang out with that crowd. I'm sure that you can get them, but I would say they are **much less prevalent here than in more liberal areas** of the country."

Q "I haven't heard or seen anything outrageous involving drugs. **If you want something, it can be found**, but it is not the predominant thing on campus. Most drugs are taken off campus anyway. Drinking happens quite a lot, though."

Q "I really **don't see a huge problem with drugs** on campus at all. Maybe I am blind, but I guess it all depends on who you become friends with. I have never been in contact with a problem, though."

Q "As far as drugs go, Columbia, in general, has a pretty big coke problem. Many of the **club and bar owners deal the stuff out the back door**, but I have not seen any violence erupt as a result of drugs being dealt. There is definitely a coke problem, though."

Q "I really don't know what to say about the drug scene other than that if you want it, **you will probably be able to somehow get your hands on it** with as many college students as there are in this city."

Q "Every college campus has its drug scene. You don't have to look very far to find someone that uses or knows someone that uses drugs. However, **it's not that sort of situation where everyone's doing it**."

The College Prowler Take On...
Drug Scene

The drug scene at USC is not highly visible, but it is there nonetheless. Marijuana is the most common drug of choice, but ecstasy and cocaine are available, as well. The prominence of the drug scene depends on the crowd a student chooses to associate with. When students do choose to get high, they usually do it in privacy with their circle of friends or at parties. You will not see anyone pressuring anyone else into doing drugs, because people are more concerned about using it for their own entertainment rather than making money by selling it. But if a student wants the drugs, they are there for the taking.

Alcohol is used more and is easier to obtain than anything else. Students of all ages drink it in the dorms, in bars, and at parties. Even those who don't drink are sometimes vexed by its consequences. Whether it's the stench of barf in the elevator because someone couldn't hold their liquor, or the loud hallmates who wake you up in the wee hours of the morning, alcohol effects everyone. There is no way to escape exposure to it, but then again, there is rarely peer pressure to drink if you don't want to. The extent of a student's exposure to drugs really depends on their friends and the atmosphere in which they live in.

B

The College Prowler® Grade on
Drug Scene: B

A high grade in the Drug Scene indicates that drugs are not a noticeable part of campus life, drug use is not visible, and no pressure to use them seems to exist.

Campus
Strictness

The Lowdown On...
Campus Strictness

What Are You Most Likely to Get Caught Doing on Campus?

- Having candles or other items not permitted in your room
- Keeping guests in the dorm past curfew
- Parking illegally
- Smoking illegal substances
- Sneaking guests into the dorm
- Underage drinking

Students Speak Out On...
Campus Strictness

> **"USC claims to be strict, but of course, there are always parties. I haven't heard any stories about people getting into trouble or thrown off campus, or anything like that."**

Q "It's a rare occurrence for faculty to get in the way of us having a good time. You have to be discreet about it if you are underage. Bring your drinks in a bag when you're going through the lobby. Get to be buds with your resident assistant (RA). **Use a blow tube when you smoke up**."

Q "**Three words: don't get caught**. Punishment for drinking is pretty strict around here. SLED (South Carolina Law Enforcement Division) loves to walk around the bars and randomly check IDs. I guess it's for everyone's own safety, though."

Q "The police are fair. If they catch you doing drugs, especially on campus, you're out of school. As far as drinking is concerned, I think that if you're not causing a problem, you're okay. It's when you're drinking at football games, using a fake ID, or going to a club when they start **fining you and giving you community service**."

Q "They really aren't that strict about drinking. I mean, if you go downtown to the bars, just be careful, because they will **give you a ticket if they catch you**. If you get caught with drugs, I'm sure that they will do something to you. So the only thing I can say about that is just don't get caught. Just be careful, and if you don't do anything stupid, you will be fine."

Q "I would say that strictness depends on who is in charge. I know **RAs that will call the cops in a second and others who are more slack**. People do get busted, but I also know there are ways around the rules for those who insist on breaking them. The cops will enforce the law. It's not really how strict they are, but how strict the RAs in the dorms are. Overall, I would not say USC is a crazy party school. If one wants to get slammed, he or she can find a party. But I would say that it is much more restrained than many campuses."

Q "They like to say they're strict, and they may enforce it at the beginning of the year, but they slack off a bit after awhile. One good thing about USC is the fraternity parties. The school also supplies busses to off-campus parties so no one drinks and drives, and it doesn't matter about the age. They basically know that there is a lot of underage drinking going on at school. **The dorms are kind of strict**. You have to be careful depending on which dorm you live in. It also depends on how cool your RA is. I think that the drug policy is zero-tolerance, though."

Q "As long as you are not loud in your dorm, you are fine drinking and doing drugs, unless your RA sucks and tries to get you in trouble. The campus police usually do not tolerate drunken behavior outside of your own dorm room, but fraternity halls, sorority halls, Preston, and all the **Honors College dorms are really cool about not getting you in trouble for drinking**."

Q "Campus **police don't mess around when it comes to substance abuse**, especially with the underage usage."

Q "The **police are not so strict on drinking**, but pretty strict on drugs."

The College Prowler Take On...
Campus Strictness

Strictness on campus is pretty moderate, and students can usually find ways to get away with things as long as they are careful. Rules are enforced directly by RAs, the USC Police Department, and the South Carolina Law Enforcement Department. The severity of the punishment often depends on who students are dealing with. RAs are generally more lenient when it comes to drug usage, and most tend not to notice or care as long as it's done discretely.

However, campus police are very strict about drugs and drinking. You can get kicked out of housing, lose your scholarship, or get kicked out of school if the police catch you with drugs. Alcohol is probably the most difficult thing for authorities to monitor, but students do get in trouble for alcohol usage from time to time, even though punishment is not as severe as it would be for usage of other drugs such as marijuana or cocaine. The main concern of authorities seems to focus on alcohol usage and that it does not get out of hand, that students are safe, and that situations involving drugs do not get out of control. As long as students are not blatantly obvious about drug usage, chances are, they will not have to worry about getting caught.

The College Prowler® Grade on

Campus Strictness: B-

A high Campus Strictness grade implies an overall lenient atmosphere; police and RAs are fairly tolerant, and the administration's rules are flexible.

Parking

The Lowdown On...
Parking

Approximate Parking Permit Cost:
$175 for a garage space
$40 for a general
　　parking permit

USC Parking Services:
(803) 777-5160
www.sc.edu/vmps

Student Parking Lot?
Yes

Freshmen Allowed to Park?
Yes

Common Parking Tickets:
Expired Meter: $5
No Parking Zone: $25
Fire Lane: $50
Handicapped Zone: $100

Parking Permits

Priority for garage spaces are given to faculty and upperclassmen. An online parking permit application can be submitted through USC's Visual Information Processing Web site at *https://vip.sc.edu*.

Did You Know?

Best Places to Find a Parking Spot

The Coliseum lot

Anywhere after 5 p.m. until 8 a.m.

Good Luck Getting a Parking Spot Here!

Metered spots

Smaller student lots located near the dorms

Students Speak Out On...
Parking

{ **"Parking is very difficult to find unless you don't mind planting your car a good mile away from your dorm room."**

Q "Parking! This is the big negative at USC. The key to happiness here is to dish out the $175 a semester and get a reserved garage space. I tried last year to pay for the $40 sticker and park in the student lots and on the street, but it is not worth it! **It will ruin many of your days**. I am told that everything is fine if you have a guaranteed spot in a garage, however."

Q "It's miserable; I won't lie. We have a severe parking shortage, and it sucks. The situation is only getting worse. We're **getting more and more students in per year, and all they do is tear up parking** spaces and put in grassy areas. Parking here is crap. You should really get a garage space if you're going to bring your car. It costs $175 a semester, but it's worth it."

Q "Parking on campus depends on if you live on or off campus. If you live on campus, then it is great. **If you live off campus, then it sucks**. There is one commuter parking lot, but there are plenty of hourly parking garages on campus that you can use."

Q "Until now, parking hasn't been that bad. There are parking lots and garages, but for some reason, they are going to **make the campus a more walker-friendly** campus. They have been gradually tearing up some parking and putting down grass."

Q "**Parking really stinks unless you get a pass** for a garage. It is $175 a semester, but trust me, it is worth it. Otherwise, you will drive around town for an hour and then end up paying the meters, which adds up. It's better to just bite the bullet, pay $175 a semester, and know that you will always have a spot."

Q "If you get a spot in the right garage (Bull Street is the best), parking isn't a problem. Sometimes, if you don't have a good spot, **walking to your garage can be a pain**. And if you live off campus and don't have a spot, it's a little difficult, too."

Q "**Buy a parking pass to park in a garage** and it will be okay. If not, good luck! You are downtown in a big city where businesses flourish, so parking does become a problem if you are not wise and don't buy a parking permit."

Q "Parking is easy if you have a parking garage sticker, but **hard if you're trying to get a metered space** or a general parking area."

Q "There's **no parking on campus**. Or, it's all really far away from anything. The best bet is a garage spot, but they are not cheap."

Q "Parking is difficult because we have such a large amount of students on campus that bring cars. But also, we have a **huge amount of commuter students that drive** onto campus every day. Parking can be hard at times. I suggest you park behind the Coliseum and then catch the Cocky Shuttle up to campus."

The College Prowler Take On...
Parking

Parking on campus at USC is absolutely atrocious. You can either get a garage space and pay over a hundred dollars for it, or you can get a $40 parking decal, but have to fight to find a space. This is one of the disadvantages of having campus in the middle of the city. Not only are students looking for parking, but so are tons of other people going downtown for work. There are nine parking garages, which cost $175 per semester, where students are guaranteed a spot. There are also parking lots where students with a decal can park. Considering the amount of students who have cars on campus, the amount of general student parking provided is not much at all.

Parking may be one of the most annoying things you will experience at USC, and it's only getting worse. There has never been a great deal of parking for students, but the school is actually in the process of reducing it on campus to make it a more walker-friendly campus, which students are quite unhappy about. Taking into account the number of students commuting and bringing their cars on campus, it's safe to say that students would be willing to sacrifice some of the pretty scenery on their way to class so that they might have a parking space.

B

The College Prowler® Grade on
Parking: B

A high grade in the Parking section indicates that parking is both available and affordable, and that parking enforcement isn't overly severe.

Transportation

The Lowdown On...
Transportation

Ways to Get Around Town:

On Campus

USC Shuttle

(803) 777-1080

Monday–Friday
7:30 a.m.–5:30 p.m.,
6 p.m.–12:30 a.m.

APO Escort Services

(803) 777-DUCK

Public Transportation

Columbia Area Transit System

(803) 748-3019

*www.ersys.com/usa/45/
4516000/ptranbus.htm*

Call or visit the Web site for a map of easy access to the public transportation system.

Taxi Cabs

AAA Taxi Service
(803) 791-7282

Blue Ribbon Taxi Cab Corp.
(803) 754-8163

➜

(Taxi Cabs. continued)

Capitol City Cab
(803) 233-8294

Checker-Yellow Cab Co., Inc.
(803) 799-3311

Classic Taxi Cab Co.
(803) 348-0662

Dennis Boyce Taxi Service
(803) 238-3377

Gamecock Cab Co.
(803) 796-7700

Car Rentals

Alamo
Local: (803) 822-5180
National: (800) 327-9633
www.alamo.com

Avis
Local: (803) 822-5100
National: (800) 831-2847
www.avis.com

Dollar
Local: (803) 822-2300
National: (800) 800-4000
www.dollar.com

Enterprise
Local: (803) 748-9214
National: (800) 736-8222
www.enterprise.com

Hertz
Local: (803) 822-8341
National: (800) 654-3131
www.hertz.com

National
Local: (803) 822-5180
National: (800) 227-7368
www.nationalcar.com

Best Ways to Get Around Town

Bike

Car

Scooter

USC Shuttle

Walk

Ways to Get Out of Town:

Airport

Columbia Metropolitan Airport
(803) 822-5000

www.columbiaairport.com

The Columbia Metropolitan Airport is seven miles and about a 15-minute drive from campus.

Airlines Serving Columbia

COMAIR
(800) 354-9822
www.comair.com

Continental
(800) 523-3273
www.continental.com

Delta
(800) 221-1212
www.delta.com

United
(800) 241-6522
www.united.com

US Airways
(800) 428-4322
www.usairways.com

How to Get to the Airport

AAA Airport Shuttle Service
(803) 796-3626

Ard's Airport Shuttle
(803) 791-5767

A cab ride to the airport costs
around $20.

Greyhound

2015 Gervais St., Columbia
(803) 256-6465
www.greyhound.com

The Greyhound Bus Terminal is
in downtown Columbia, about
one mile from campus.

Amtrak

950 Pulaski St., Columbia
(803) 252-8246
www.amtrak.com

The Amtrak Train Station is in
downtown Columbia, about
two miles from campus.

Travel Agents

AAA Vacations
810 Dutch Square Blvd.
(803) 798-9205

Columbia Travel and Tours Inc.
224 O'Neil Ct.
(803) 788-7111

Elim Travel Agency
1612 Main St.
(803) 933-9601

Pal Travel
2301 Beltline Blvd.
(803) 787-5530

Piedmont Travel
1931 Bull St.
(803) 765-1212

Students Speak Out On...
Transportation

> **"I wouldn't recommend the public transportation—those public buses are rather scary if you ask me."**

Q "Public transportation is very convenient. Shuttles are available to take you from one area of the campus to another. Because it is so large, and some dorms are very far from some of the classes you may take, this may be an option for you. It's all very accessible, but **even though transportation is pretty easy, most people walk**, unless you're lazy."

Q "The **public transportation system here stinks**; it isn't very good. And if you stayed on campus, you could easily walk to anything that you needed to get to downtown. If, however, you wanted to go to the mall, you'd need a car. If you didn't bring your car, though, I'm sure that someone in your hall would be more than willing to go or let you borrow theirs. There is a bus transportation system on campus that is very convenient."

Q "**USC has its own bus system**, and the city of Columbia provides public buses as well. Our buses drive on campus and take you to the main spots. I have used the bus system on campus, and it is really good."

Q "Some people take cabs from Five Points, but they're a little expensive. There's a city bus, but it doesn't really visit campus. It's definitely a convenience to have your own car, but I **didn't have a car my freshman year, and I did just fine**."

Q "I wouldn't be caught dead on one of those buses, but the campus does have shuttle buses that are pretty reliable. Also, **at night they have vans that drive you around campus** or to Five Points, but if you don't have your own car, make friends with someone who does very quickly. You don't really need to go anywhere off campus, but it's always good to know someone who can spare you the hassle of public transportation."

Q "The **school has about four different buses** all around campus that make different stops for classes, dorms, and all that. I don't really know about city transportation since I've never taken it."

Q "I would only **recommend using the USC shuttle**, which reaches every corner of USC's campus that spreads across downtown Columbia. As for traveling around Columbia in general, it's almost necessary for an individual to have access to a car for a Wal-Mart run or even just to get to the coffee shop. If you live on campus, this normally isn't a problem if someone on your hall has a vehicle."

Q "The **Cock Shuttle is pretty good**; it gets you to and from the major spots on campus. Columbia city buses are not safe, and I would not allow my friends to ride them."

Q "The transportation system is okay, I guess; **they really need more shuttles**. If you miss it, then you're going to be very late."

The College Prowler Take On...
Transportation

The public transportation system in Columbia is actually quite comprehensive, and students have a number of options to get around. The city has convenient buses for students going off campus. Some say that they are unsafe, but they are probably just as safe as other cities the size of Columbia. But, students should never travel around by themselves at night. The Carolina Shuttles traverse campus and are helpful for students trying to get from one end of campus to another. It only takes about 15–20 minutes to walk from one end of campus to the other, but if a student is in a rush to get to class, or just doesn't feel like walking, the shuttle can be pretty convenient. Taxis are available if students want to use them, but most don't because they usually find cheaper ways to get where they want to go.

To get out of town without a car, there is an Amtrak station, a Greyhound bus station, and the Columbia Metropolitan Airport, all relatively close to campus. Students find these convenient, especially if they live far away. The easiest way to get from around campus is to walk or ride a bike. Bike racks are located outside almost every building on campus. At USC, there are a number of relatively inexpensive and convenient ways to get around, whether you're going out of town or just across campus.

A-

The College Prowler® Grade on

Transportation: A-

A high grade for Transportation indicates that campus buses, public buses, cabs, and rental cars are readily-available and affordable. Other determining factors include proximity to an airport and the necessity of transportation.

Weather

The Lowdown On...
Weather

Average Temperature:

Fall:	66 °F
Winter:	47 °F
Spring:	66 °F
Summer:	84 °F

Average Precipitation:

Fall:	3.96 in.
Winter:	4.17 in.
Spring:	4.55 in.
Summer:	4.42 in.

Students Speak Out On...
Weather

> **"The weather is awesome. Most of the year it doesn't drop below 70 degrees, and the winter is very short and fairly mild."**

 "The **summer is really hot**. If you don't like hot weather, South Carolina might not be the place for you."

Q "Just warning you now, it is hot and humid during the summer. It is extremely comfortable during the fall, just as it is in the spring. During the winter, the average temperature is probably in the 50s. With Columbia being in the middle of the state, **the beach and the mountains are both only about two hours away**."

Q "Columbia is **scorching during the summer** and usually around 90 to 95 degrees. It is pleasant in the fall for Gamecock football, and it is usually around 50 degrees in the winter. Spring is pleasant as well; it's normally in the 70s."

Q "**Prepare for hurricanes**, but they don't do anything besides get you out of school. Columbia is inland, so you will be pretty safe here."

Q "The weather in South Carolina is awesome! It is one of the primary reasons I came to school here. I can wear shorts for 10 months out of the year, **it doesn't rain a lot**, and the only time it is prohibitively hot is in the middle of the summer."

Q "**The weather is gorgeous**. It doesn't get too cold in the winters, and I love warm weather. We get a little snow, but nothing major at all. And to be honest, we normally never get snow. I think the coldest it normally gets is somewhere in the mid-40s, and that is very rare!"

Q "Weather here in SC is hot in the summer, rainy (not thunderstorms—just drizzle and downpour all day) sometimes for days on end, and **mild winters (prepare for snow, but not blizzards)**."

Q "Summertime is hot, sunny, and humid. Lotion up, and put on the tank tops, shorts, and shades. Winter is usually mild, and if you're lucky, school will be cancelled for a day because of the threat of snow. That's right—southerners are **not accustomed to any sort of winter wonderland**."

Q "It's usually **hot and not too cold**, but sometimes it gets abnormally cold."

Q "You should **bring all of your summer clothing** because it gets very hot and humid, but also bring a winter jacket and a pair of hiking boots in case of the occasion of snow."

Q "The **coldest weather we have is usually in January**, and the school will close if we have a quarter of an inch of snow on the ground. The weather is usually pleasant for most of the school year, with it being very warm/hot in August, September, April, and May."

Q "The weather is very hot! **Columbia is always humid**— bring a variety of clothing, but be sure to bring your bathing suit!"

The College Prowler Take On...
Weather

The weather at Carolina is really hot and humid in the summer and mild in the winter. Pollen season covers the campus with a blanket of yellow, which can be pretty heinous for people with allergy problems, so bring allergy medicine if you need to. Shorts, T-shirts, and tank tops are must-haves. And if you're not bashful, you might want to bring your bathing suit because many students like to tan on the Horseshoe when the weather is really nice.

The winters don't get very cold, but you will need to bring some warm clothes—a coat, boots, sweaters, and warm pants. Some students wear gloves, scarves, and hats during the winter, but you will also see students walking around in flip-flops in the middle of January. It just depends on what kind of climate you're used to. Sometimes, it snows, but usually that happens only once or twice a year. Even then, it's usually less than an inch, but that means a definite cancellation of classes at least for one day. Most of the time, the weather in Columbia is beautiful, sunny, and maybe a little sweltering, but students agree that it's one of the things that makes going to USC so enjoyable.

The College Prowler® Grade on

Weather: B+

A high Weather grade designates that temperatures are mild and rarely reach extremes, that the campus tends to be sunny rather than rainy, and that weather is fairly consistent rather than unpredictable.

Report Card Summary

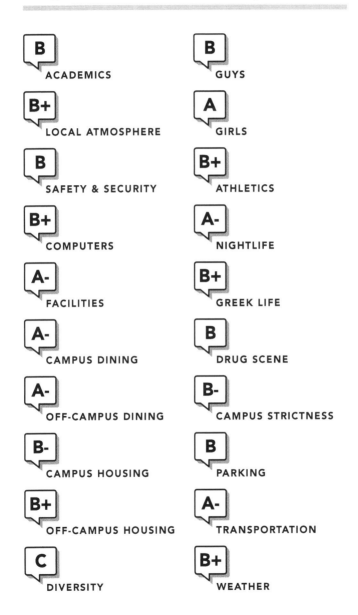

B ACADEMICS

B GUYS

B+ LOCAL ATMOSPHERE

A GIRLS

B SAFETY & SECURITY

B+ ATHLETICS

B+ COMPUTERS

A- NIGHTLIFE

A- FACILITIES

B+ GREEK LIFE

A- CAMPUS DINING

B DRUG SCENE

A- OFF-CAMPUS DINING

B- CAMPUS STRICTNESS

B- CAMPUS HOUSING

B PARKING

B+ OFF-CAMPUS HOUSING

A- TRANSPORTATION

C DIVERSITY

B+ WEATHER

Overall Experience

Students Speak Out On...
Overall Experience

{ **"I would have to say the past three years at USC have most certainly been a learning experience. I don't think I would have rather gone anywhere else."**

Q "I am going to be a senior, and I sometimes wish I would have chosen a different school. But overall, I love it. I have had **some of the best memories here**, and I don't think I would want to be anywhere else. But, we always say that when it comes to South Carolina, you either hate it or you love it."

Q "I've really enjoyed my transition to South Carolina. There is **a lot of school spirit and plenty of nice people** on campus to help you with problems or whatever the case may be. It's a really nice place to be. I guess I haven't heard any bad comments from anyone, and I think that I am going to an awesome and very unique school. I have really enjoyed my time here."

Q "My overall opinion about USC is that it is an awesome school. I have been to a couple of different schools, and this is definitely the happiest I have been. I am glad I came here, and I have no regrets. **USC has an excellent academic reputation**, which is a big reason why I came here."

Q "I would never consider going anywhere but USC. I love it with all my heart. People in South Carolina are really kind. The **campus is beautiful, with oaks, ponds, palmettos, and gardens**. It is truly a special place. USC has over 20,000 students, but you cannot go two feet without seeing someone you know. I would highly recommend that you become a Gamecock and come to USC. With all the new buildings and developments that are going on, it is an exciting time to be a Gamecock."

Q "I actually wish I would have gone somewhere else. Columbia is a lot of fun for the first couple of years because **football is really fun, and the weather is nice** most of the time. People at this school are pretty fun, too. However, now I am tired of it and really wish I had not gone here."

Q "I think that this is a great school. It's a place where **I feel truly at home**. The people here are extremely friendly and welcoming, which is nice. I visited over 12 schools before I decided to come here, and I now know from spending the past year here that I couldn't have chosen a better school or city."

Q "To be honest, I like USC. In-state tuition is a **good deal for a school of its size and caliber**. I've really enjoyed the past few years here, and I wouldn't take them back. I've enjoyed being educated here."

Q "I wish I would have come here from the start. Whatever you are into, there is something for you here. If you're into the beach, it's one hour away. The mountains are two hours away, and skiing is four hours away, but you never want to leave because there is always something going on. As for the cost, I think that this is **one of the cheapest universities out of all the state schools**. The cost of living is not ridiculous either."

Q "I love USC. Along with receiving a great education, I've **made friends for life**."

Q "I love Carolina. I have met so many great people from all over the country, and even people that lived 10 minutes from me who I hadn't met until I came here. In spite of it being such a large campus, I really feel **I have had a personal experience at Carolina**."

Q "I have had a really good experience here, but it seems to me that the most **important element that dictates your happiness at college is the friends you make**. I have met some great people, built lifelong friendships, and I've also learned a lot."

The College Prowler Take On...
Overall Experience

If there is one word to describe the experiences you will have at USC, it would have to be unforgettable. Being away from home for the first time is one of the things that makes it so exciting, and even a bit scary at times. But the freedom you get when you come here just feels so natural that it makes you wonder why they don't send people to college sooner! Academically, there are courses and teachers who can make you look at things in ways you never considered before and literally change your outlook. The professors will fill you with facts and figures, but some of them can teach you a lot about life as well. And on top of this, with such a large student population, you will inevitably form new relationships, even some that will last a lifetime.

As at any college, the quality of the experience depends on what you put into it. There are thousands of new people to meet, there are activities going on, and there are things to learn both in and out of class. But those who don't take advantage of these opportunities will not get a lot out of their experience here. Some students get tired of being at USC after a while, and some hate it from the start for whatever reason. USC is not the place for everyone. But overall, students seem to be thoroughly enamored with Carolina and wouldn't trade their title of Gamecocks for anything in the world.

The Inside Scoop

The Lowdown On...
The Inside Scoop

USC Slang:

Know the slang, know the school. The following is a list of things you really need to know before coming to USC. The more of these words you know, the better off you'll be.

BA Building – The Business Administration building or Hipp-Close building.

Blackboard – An online tool that students and teachers use for assignments and discussions on class topics.

Five Points – An area of Columbia where many students go to find a drink or a good place to eat; you can get there from campus by heading down Green Street.

The Gimp – Short for Grand Market Place (GMP); the cafeteria on the first floor of the Russell House.

The Horseshoe – USC's central lawn on campus.

The New Gym – Strom Thurmond Fitness and Wellness Center on Assembly Street.

The Old Gym – The Blatt PE Center on Wheat Street.

The Quads – South Quad and East Quad are upper-class, apartment-style dorms.

RHD – Residence Hall Director.

SLED – South Carolina Law Enforcement Department

The Towers – Freshman dorms Douglas, LaBorde, Moore, and Snowden.

USCPD – University of South Carolina Police Department.

VIP – Visual Information Processing; Web site where students can pay tuition, register for classes, look at their transcript.

The Vista – A strip of restaurants and bars on Gervais Street.

Things I Wish I Knew Before Coming to USC

- Avoid crowds at the bookstore, and don't wait until the last minute to buy your books.

- It's normal for freshmen to be undecided about their majors, so don't stress about it.

- Buy a reserved garage space.

- Get involved in some organization because it's a great way to make friends.

- Use the UCHOOSE online system to find a roommate.

- Don't blend in! At such a big campus, you can get lost in the crowd. Make sure your professors, advisors, and RAs know who you are.

Tips to Succeed at USC

- Be prepared before going for advisement because the advisors don't always know what they're talking about.

- Research professors before registering for class.

- Go to class and actually pay attention.

- Get to know your professors.

- Plan ahead by researching and applying for scholarships and internships as soon as possible—talk to counselors in the Career Center.

School Spirit

Students at USC are teeming with school spirit, especially during football season. USC T-shirts, shorts, bumper stickers, and caps are seen all around the city of Columbia, as both students and alumni display their pride at being a member of the USC community. There are many reasons that students love USC, but sports are the main reason that they display such pride. You will never see students come together the way they do before a big football game here at USC.

Traditions

First Night Carolina

The night after moving in, don't be surprised if you see hundreds of students bunched in front of the Russell House and shuttle buses lined up for blocks down Green Street. This is part of First Night Carolina, an opportunity for freshmen to get to know each other, and a way for USC to welcome them to the college. Students are transported by shuttle bus to a secret location where a special program awaits them, which usually involves free food and loud music. It is a great way for students to get involved on their first night away from home, and also gives them a chance to meet new people.

Shopping Day

At the end of every semester, the USC Honors College holds a Shopping Day. This is usually useful to freshmen and sophomores who have last priority on classes and are unable to register for a class because it is full. If an opening in the class becomes available after the Honors College registration deadline, students have the opportunity to vie for that spot on Shopping Day on a first-come, first-serve basis. The office opens at 8 a.m., but often, there are several students who camp out in order to ensure their place in line. Students do anything to pass the time—play games, read, sleep—and in the end, they usually get the classes they want and meet some new people at the same time.

(Traditions, continued)

Tiger Burn

The week before the big Clemson/USC football game, the University holds a variety of activities to get the students excited about the huge rivalry. One of these events is the Tiger Burn pep rally where the cheerleaders, pep band, and students come out to get pumped up about the big game. It is during this time of the year that school spirit is at its greatest. Even though all students may not be able to get tickets to the game itself, it gives them even more incentive to come to Tiger Burn and revel in the prospect of smoking the Clemson Tigers.

Top of Carolina

On Sunday mornings, the rotating restaurant on top of Capstone opens for a Sunday brunch. The brunch features an all-you-can-eat buffet, including a belgian waffle station, omelet station, a hot buffet line, and other items to choose from. Just as impressive is the amazing view of downtown Columbia from the top of an 18-story building. Reservations are available from 10:30 a.m.–1:30 p.m. and can be made by calling (803) 777-0848.

Finding a Job or Internship

The Lowdown On...
Finding a Job or Internship

One of the things that will preoccupy you the most as you approach graduation is the question of whether or not, after all the years of schooling and preparation, you will actually be able to find the job of your dream. This is why USC hires people to help students find jobs and internships, and provides services to ensure that the transition from college to the workplace is as smooth as possible.

Advice

While the staff at the Career Center is there to help, it is your job to make the effort of going there, taking the time to speak to them, and letting them help you. An early start is always the key to finding a job when the time comes, and if the people at the Career Center already know who you are, it will make your life a whole lot easier.

Career Center Resources and Services

Career counseling, career library resources, cooperative education, discovery tools, events credentials services, graduate school preparation, internships, job fairs, job postings, job shadowing, mock interviews, on-campus interviewing, resume referral, tip sheets, USC careerlink, Web resources

Firms That Most Frequently Hire Grads

Engineering firms, education, financial institutions, government, information technology companies, marketing and sales, non-profit organizations

Alumni

The Lowdown On...
Alumni

Web Site:
www.sc.edu/usc/alumni.html

Services Available:
Alumni online directory
Career Center services

Major Alumni Events

Homecoming in October, class reunions

Alumni Publications

USC Times – A publication for USC faculty, staff, and friends of the University

Did You Know?

Famous USC Alums

Andrew Card Jr. – White House Cheif-of-Staff to President George W. Bush

Alex English – Basketball Hall of Famer

Leeza Gibbons – Television celebrity

Charles Frazier – Author of *Cold Mountain* and National Book Award winner

Jim Hoagland – *Washington Post* senior foreign correspondent and two-time Pulitzer Prize winner

Hootie and the Blowfish – Grammy Award-winning musicians

Robert C. McNair – Entrepreneur, philanthropist, and owner of the Houston Texans NFL team

Dan Reeves – Former NFL head coach for the Atlanta Falcons and Denver Broncos

Marva Smalls – Executive Vice President of Nickelodeon

Student Organizations

360 Campus Ministries

Academic Team

Academy of Students
of Pharmacy

African American Student
Nurses Network

Alumni Association Student
Advisory Board

American Chemical Society

American Choral
Directors Association

American Institute of
Chemical Engineers

American Marketing
Association

American Society for
Engineering Education

American Society of
Health-System Pharmacists

American Society of
Heating, Refrigerating
and A/C Engineers

American Society of
Mechanical Engineers

American String
Teachers Association

Anthropology
Student Association

Archival Students Guild

Association of African
American Students

Association of
Computer Machinery

Baha'i Club

Baptist Collegiate Ministry

Bisexual Gay &
Lesbian Alliance

Black Law Students
Association

Blue and Gold Society

Brothers and Sisters
in Control

Brothers of Nubian Descent

Campus Advance

Campus Crusade for Christ

Canterbury of Columbia

Carolina Association of
Student Trainers

Carolina Bodybuilding
and Fitness Club

Carolina Crew

Carolina Debate

Carolina Productions

Carolina Racquetball

Carolina Student
Association for the Education
of Young Children

Carolina Television

Chi Alpha
Christian Fellowship

Chi Eta Phi –
Community Service

Chic Naissance
Fashion Society

Chinese Student's
Christian Fellowship

Christian Pharmacists
Fellowship International

Christ's Student
Church at Carolina

Civil Air Patrol Air
Force ROTC

Club Manager's Association
of America

College of Pharmacy
Student Government

Comparative Literature
Student Association

Creative Music and
Film Society

Criminal Justice Association

Criminal Law Society

Cycling Club of the University
of South Carolina

Dance Company

Delta Sigma Pi – Business

Doctoral Student Association

Ducks Unlimited at USC

Environmental Law Society

Family of African American
Pre-Med Students

Fashion Board

Federal Bar Association
Student Chapter

Federalist Society

Fellowship
Contemporary Society

Fellowship of
Christian Athletes

Fencing Club

Field Hockey Club

Filipino American
Student Association

Financial Management
Association

The Forum – Law Newspaper

Friendship Association
of Chinese Students
and Scholars

Gamecock Dance Sport
Ballroom Dancing

Gamecock – Student
Newspaper

Gamecocks Advocating
Mature Management
of Alcohol

Garnet & Black Magazine

Geography Club

Geography Graduate
Student Association

Geology Club

German Club

Graduate Association
of Biological Sciences

Graduate Student
Association

Graphic Artists Association

Health Law Society

Healthcare Executive
Student Association

Higher Harmony

Hillel

Hindu Students Council

Hong Kong
Student Association

Ice Hockey Club

IMBA Student Association

Indian Cultural Exchange

Indian Student Organization

Information Technology
Organization

Institute of Electrical and
Electronic Engineers

Intellectual Property
Law Society

InterAct at USC

International Business
Student Association

International Food Services
Executives Association

International Friendship
Ministries

International Law Society

International Student
Association

InterVarsity
Christian Fellowship

Judo Club

Kappa Epsilon – Pharmacy

Karate Self-Defense Club

Korean Students Association

Lacrosse Club

Latter-day Saint
Student Association

Library and Information
Science Student Association

Lutheran Campus Ministry

Marine Science
Graduate Society

Marine Science
Undergraduate Society

Master of Accountancy/
Taxation Association

Master of Business
Administration Student
Association

Master of International
Business Student Association

Master of Public
Administration
Student Association

Medical Graduate
Student Association

Medical Student Association

Men's Soccer Club

Mock Trial Team

Mountaineering and
Whitewater Club

Multicultural Health Council

Music Educators
National Conference

Muslim Students Association

NAACP

NASHI Anime Club

National Association of
Black Journalists

National Science
Teachers Association

National Society of
Black Engineers

National Student
Exchange Association

National Student
Speech Language
Hearing Association

National Wild
Turkey Federation

Net Impact – Corporate
Social Responsibility

Newman Club

Nichiren Buddhist Club

Optical Society of America

Orthodox Christian
Fellowship

PALM Campus Ministr

Palmetto Chapter of
Professional Convention
Managers Association

Phi Alpha Delta – Law

Phi Mu Alpha – Music

Physics Graduate
Student Associatio

Presbyterian Student
Association

Promoting, Educating,
and Encouraging
Realistic Self-Image

Psychology Graduate
Student Association

Public Relations Student
Society of America

Puppet Regime Independent
Theatre Group

Reformed University
Fellowship

Residence Hall Association

Roller Hockey Club

Romanian Student
Association of USC

Rugby Team

Round Table Gaming Society

Russian Club

SAVVY

SC Trial Lawyers Association

Scuba Club

Seidokan Aikido Club

Semper Fidelis Society
Marine Corps

The Shack Christian Ministries

Shandon College Ministry

Social Work
Student Association

Society for Human
Resource Management

Society for the Advancement
Of the Chemical Sciences

Society of
Automotive Engineers

Society for Hispanic
Professional Engineers

Society of Women Engineers

South Carolina
Education Association

South Carolina Honors
College Council

South Carolina
Student Legislature

Sport Administration Club

Sports and Entertainment
Law Society

Spurgeon Foundation
Ministry

Statistics Club

Student Advertising
Federation

Student Bar Association

Student Christian Fellowship

Student Gamecock Club

Student National
Pharmaceutical Association

Student Nurses Association

Student Pagan Inter-Religious
Awareness League

Student Personnel
Association

Students Allied for a
Greener Earth

Students Associated for
Latin America

Students Educating and
Empowering for Diversity

Students for Life

Students Together in
Networking Graduates

Thelion Quizbowl Society

Three Rivers Literary Journal

Turkish Student Association

Ultimate Frisbee Club

Undergraduate Council in
Religion & Classics

Undergraduate Council of
Gender and Women's Studies

Undergraduate
Economics Council

Undergraduate Film &
Media Studies Council

Undergraduate
History Council

Undergraduate
Musicians' Council

Undergraduate
Neuroscience Council

Undergraduate Political
Science Council

Up Til Dawn – Community
Service Project

Vietnamese Student
Organization

Volleyball Club

Water Polo Club

Waterski Club

Wesley Foundation –
Methodist Church

Women Students Association

Women's Lacrosse Club

Women's Rugby

Women's Soccer Club

World Tae Kwon Do Club

WUSC FM

Young Life of Columbia

The Best
& Worst

The Ten **BEST** Things About USC

1 Football games

2 Cocky the mascot and Cocks paraphernalia

3 International Business School

4 Honors College

5 Strom Thurmond Fitness and Wellness Center

6 Carolina Center

7 The Horseshoe

8 Cute guys and girls

9 High-speed Internet access

10 Free movies at the Russell House

The Ten **WORST** Things About USC

1 Parking

2 Tuition increases

3 Closed-minded people

4 Hot summers

5 Incompetent advisors

6 Diversity (or lack thereof)

7 Did I mention parking?

8 Long lines

9 Community bathrooms

10 Huge lecture classes

Visiting

The Lowdown On...
Visiting

Hotel Information:

Downtown:

Adam's Mark
1200 Hampton St., Columbia
(800) 444-2326
www.adamsmark.com
Distance from Campus:
Less than a mile
Price Range: $100–$140
*Be sure to ask for USC rate
when making reservations

**Best Western
Governors House Hotel**
1301 Main St., Columbia
(803) 779-7790
www.bestwestern.com
Distance from Campus:
Less than a mile
Price Range: $74–$129

Clarion Townhouse
1615 Gervais St., Columbia
(803) 771-8711
(800) 277-8711

(Clarion, continued)

www.clariontownhouse.com
Distance from Campus:
Less than a mile
Price Range: $89–$135
*Be sure to ask for USC rate
when making reservations

Comfort Suites Downtown

501 Taylor St., Columbia
(803) 744-4000
www.comfortsuites.com
Distance from Campus:
1.1 miles
Price Range: $100–$160

Holiday Inn Coliseum

630 Assembly St., Columbia
(803) 799-7800
www.holiday-inn.com
Distance from Campus:
Less than a mile
Price Range: $85–$145
*Be sure to ask for USC rate
when making reservations

Rose Hall Bed & Breakfast

1006 Barnwell St., Columbia
(803) 771-2288
www.rosehallbb.com
Distance from Campus:
Less than a mile
Price Range: $90–$140
*Be sure to ask for USC rate
when making reservations

Five Points Area:

Claussens Inn

2003 Greene St., Columbia
(800) 622-3382
www.claussensinn.com
Distance from Campus:
Less than a mile
Price Range: $125–$140

The Whitney

700 Woodrow St., Columbia
(803) 252-0845
www.whitneyhotel.com
Distance from Campus:
1.3 miles
Price Range: $110–$160

St. Andrews Area:

Courtyard Columbia Northwest

347 Zimalcrest Dr., Columbia
(803) 731-2300
(800) 321-2211
www.marriott.com
Distance from Campus:
7.9 miles
Price Range: $75–$150
*Be sure to ask for USC rate
when making reservations.

Days Inn Central Columbia

911 Bush River Rd., Columbia
(803) 798-5101
www.daysinn.com
Distance from Campus:
4.7 miles
Price Range: $45–$65

Residence Inn Columbia

150 Stoneridge Dr., Columbia

(803) 779-7000

www.marriott.com/residenceinn

Distance from Campus:
3.2 miles

Price Range: $75–$190

Northeast Columbia Area:

Ramada Plaza Hotel

8105 Two Notch Rd., Columbia

(803) 736-5600
(800) 2-RAMADA

www.ramada.com

Distance from Campus:
7.8 miles

Price Range: $65–$80

*Be sure to ask for USC rate when making reservations.

West Columbia Area:

Best Western

650 Cherokee Ln.
West Columbia

(803) 796-9400

www.bestwestern.com

Distance from Campus:
3.2 miles

Price Range: $50–$60

Take a Campus Virtual Tour

www.sc.edu/horseshoe

To Schedule a Group Information Session or Interview

Call the Visitor Center at (800) 922-9755

Monday–Friday 8:30 a.m.–5 p.m.
Saturday 9:30 a.m.–12:30 p.m. (May–August)

Campus Tours

The Visitors Center generally offers guided walking tours Monday through Friday. Tours last approximately two hours and continue regardless of weather (so be prepared and dress appropriately). The Center recommends that you submit a campus visit request at least two weeks prior to your visit. If you are planning a visit for a school, civic, or other special group, visit requests must be made over the phone by calling the Visitor Center.

Tours depart Monday–Friday at 10 a.m. and 2 p.m. and on Saturday at 10 a.m. September–May and Monday–Friday at 10 a.m June–August.

Call (800) 922-9755 or visit *http://visitorcenter.sc.edu.*

Directions to Campus

Driving from the North

- Take I-77 South and exit onto SC 277 toward Columbia.

- Stay on this freeway which becomes Bull Street. Follow Bull Street until it intersects with Pendleton Street.

- Turn right onto Pendleton Street and proceed four blocks until you get to Assembly Street.

- Turn left onto Assembly Street and USC's Visitor Center will be on your immediate right.

Driving from the South

- Take US 76/378, which will change from Sumter Highway to Garners Ferry Road to Devine Street. Devine will intersect with Harden Street at Five Points.

- Turn left onto Harden Street and take the next right onto Blossom Street.

- Turn right at the sixth stoplight onto Assembly Street. The Visitor Center will be 4 blocks ahead on your left.

Driving from the East

Via I-20

- Take I-20 West and turn off at SC 277 (Exit 73) toward Columbia.

- Stay on this freeway which becomes Bull Street.

- Follow Bull Street until it intersects with Pendleton Street.

- Turn right onto Pendleton Street and proceed four blocks until you get to Assembly Street.

- Turn left onto Assembly Street and USC's Visitor Center will be on your immediate right.

(Driving from the East, continued)

Via I-26

- Take I-26 West and turn off at exit 111-B (US 1) and continue until you see the Congaree River. The street name changes from Meeting Street to Gervais Street.
- Continue several blocks. At the South Carolina State Capitol, turn right onto Assembly Street.
- The Visitor Center is two blocks on your right, just past Pendleton Street.

Driving from the West

Via I-20

- Take I-20 East and turn off at Exit 58 (US 1 toward West Columbia) and stay on this highway which becomes Meeting Street, and then becomes Gervais Street after you cross the Congaree River.
- Turn right onto Assembly Street at the South Carolina State Capitol.
- The Visitor Center will be on your right at the second traffic light.

Via I-26

- Take I-26 East and follow I-126/US 76 toward downtown Columbia and exit at Elmwood Avenue.
- Turn right onto Assembly Street and continue for 11 blocks.
- The Visitor Center will be on your right, just past Pendleton Street.

Words to Know

Academic Probation – A suspension imposed on a student if he or she fails to keep up with the school's minimum academic requirements. Those unable to improve their grades after receiving this warning can face dismissal.

Beer Pong/Beirut – A drinking game involving cups of beer arranged in a pyramid shape on each side of a table. The goal is to get a ping pong ball into one of the opponent's cups by throwing the ball or hitting it with a paddle. If the ball lands in a cup, the opponent is required to drink the beer.

Bid – An invitation from a fraternity or sorority to 'pledge' (join) that specific house.

Blue-Light Phone – Brightly-colored phone posts with a blue light bulb on top. These phones exist for security purposes and are located at various outside locations around most campuses. In an emergency, a student can pick up one of these phones (free of charge) to connect with campus police or a security escort.

Campus Police – Police who are specifically assigned to a given institution. Campus police are typically not regular city officers; they are employed by the university in a full-time capacity.

Club Sports – A level of sports that falls somewhere between varsity and intramural. If a student is unable to commit to a varsity team but has a lot of passion for athletics, a club sport could be a better, less intense option. Even less demanding, intramural (IM) sports often involve no traveling and considerably less time.

Cocaine – An illegal drug. Also known as "coke" or "blow," cocaine often resembles a white crystalline or powdery substance. It is highly addictive and dangerous.

Common Application – An application with which students can apply to multiple schools.

Course Registration – The period of official class selection for the upcoming quarter or semester. Prior to registration, it is best to prepare several back-up courses in case a particular class becomes full. If a course is full, students can place themselves on the waitlist, although this still does not guarantee entry.

Division Athletics – Athletic classifications range from Division I to Division III. Division IA is the most competitive, while Division III is considered to be the least competitive.

Dorm – A dorm (or dormitory) is an on-campus housing facility. Dorms can provide a range of options from suite-style rooms to more communal options that include shared bathrooms. Most first-year students live in dorms. Some upperclassmen who wish to stay on campus also choose this option.

Early Action – An application option with which a student can apply to a school and receive an early acceptance response without a binding commitment. This system is becoming less and less available.

Early Decision – An application option that students should use only if they are certain they plan to attend the school in question. If a student applies using the early decision option and is admitted, he or she is required and bound to attend that university. Admission rates are usually higher among students who apply through early decision, as the student is clearly indicating that the school is his or her first choice.

Ecstasy – An illegal drug. Also known as "E" or "X," ecstasy looks like a pill and most resembles an aspirin. Considered a party drug, ecstasy is very dangerous and can be deadly.

Ethernet – An extremely fast Internet connection available in most university-owned residence halls. To use an Ethernet connection properly, a student will need a network card and cable for his or her computer.

Fake ID – A counterfeit identification card that contains false information. Most commonly, students get fake IDs with altered birthdates so that they appear to be older than 21 (and therefore of legal drinking age). Even though it is illegal, many college students have fake IDs in hopes of purchasing alcohol or getting into bars.

Frosh – Slang for "freshman" or "freshmen."

Hazing – Initiation rituals administered by some fraternities or sororities as part of the pledging process. Many universities have outlawed hazing due to its degrading, and sometimes dangerous, nature.

Intramurals (IMs) – A popular, and usually free, sport league in which students create teams and compete against one another. These sports vary in competitiveness and can include a range of activities—everything from billiards to water polo. IM sports are a great way to meet people with similar interests.

Keg – Officially called a half-barrel, a keg contains roughly 200 12-ounce servings of beer.

LSD – An illegal drug, also known as acid, this hallucinogenic drug most commonly resembles a tab of paper.

Marijuana – An illegal drug, also known as weed or pot; along with alcohol, marijuana is one of the most commonly-found drugs on campuses across the country.

Major –The focal point of a student's college studies; a specific topic that is studied for a degree. Examples of majors include physics, English, history, computer science, economics, business, and music. Many students decide on a specific major before arriving on campus, while others are simply "undecided" until declaring a major. Those who are extremely interested in two areas can also choose to double major.

Meal Block – The equivalent of one meal. Students on a meal plan usually receive a fixed number of meals per week. Each meal, or "block," can be redeemed at the school's dining facilities in place of cash. Often, a student's weekly allotment of meal blocks will be forfeited if not used.

Minor – An additional focal point in a student's education. Often serving as a complement or addition to a student's main area of focus, a minor has fewer requirements and prerequisites to fulfill than a major. Minors are not required for graduation from most schools; however some students who want to explore many different interests choose to pursue both a major and a minor.

Mushrooms – An illegal drug. Also known as "'shrooms," this drug resembles regular mushrooms but is extremely hallucinogenic.

Off-Campus Housing – Housing from a particular landlord or rental group that is not affiliated with the university. Depending on the college, off-campus housing can range from extremely popular to non-existent. Students who choose to live off campus are typically given more freedom, but they also have to deal with possible subletting scenarios, furniture, bills, and other issues. In addition to these factors, rental prices and distance often affect a student's decision to move off campus.

Office Hours – Time that teachers set aside for students who have questions about coursework. Office hours are a good forum for students to go over any problems and to show interest in the subject material.

Pledging – The early phase of joining a fraternity or sorority, pledging takes place after a student has gone through rush and received a bid. Pledging usually lasts between one and two semesters. Once the pledging period is complete and a particular student has done everything that is required to become a member, that student is considered a brother or sister. If a fraternity or a sorority would decide to "haze" a group of students, this initiation would take place during the pledging period.

Private Institution – A school that does not use tax revenue to subsidize education costs. Private schools typically cost more than public schools and are usually smaller.

Prof – Slang for "professor."

Public Institution – A school that uses tax revenue to subsidize education costs. Public schools are often a good value for in-state residents and tend to be larger than most private colleges.

Quarter System (or Trimester System) – A type of academic calendar system. In this setup, students take classes for three academic periods. The first quarter usually starts in late September or early October and concludes right before Christmas. The second quarter usually starts around early to mid–January and finishes up around March or April. The last academic quarter, or "third quarter," usually starts in late March or early April and finishes up in late May or Mid-June. The fourth quarter is summer. The major difference between the quarter system and semester system is that students take more, less comprehensive courses under the quarter calendar.

RA (Resident Assistant) – A student leader who is assigned to a particular floor in a dormitory in order to help to the other students who live there. An RA's duties include ensuring student safety and providing assistance wherever possible.

Recitation – An extension of a specific course; a review session. Some classes, particularly large lectures, are supplemented with mandatory recitation sessions that provide a relatively personal class setting.

Rolling Admissions – A form of admissions. Most commonly found at public institutions, schools with this type of policy continue to accept students throughout the year until their class sizes are met. For example, some schools begin accepting students as early as December and will continue to do so until April or May.

Room and Board – This figure is typically the combined cost of a university-owned room and a meal plan.

Room Draw/Housing Lottery – A common way to pick on-campus room assignments for the following year. If a student decides to remain in university-owned housing, he or she is assigned a unique number that, along with seniority, is used to determine his or her housing for the next year.

Rush – The period in which students can meet the brothers and sisters of a particular chapter and find out if a given fraternity or sorority is right for them. Rushing a fraternity or a sorority is not a requirement at any school. The goal of rush is to give students who are serious about pledging a feel for what to expect.

Semester System – The most common type of academic calendar system at college campuses. This setup typically includes two semesters in a given school year. The fall semester starts around the end of August or early September and concludes before winter vacation. The spring semester usually starts in mid-January and ends in late April or May.

Student Center/Rec Center/Student Union – A common area on campus that often contains study areas, recreation facilities, and eateries. This building is often a good place to meet up with fellow students; depending on the school, the student center can have a huge role or a non-existent role in campus life.

Student ID – A university-issued photo ID that serves as a student's key to school-related functions. Some schools require students to show these cards in order to get into dorms, libraries, cafeterias, and other facilities. In addition to storing meal plan information, in some cases, a student ID can actually work as a debit card and allow students to purchase things from bookstores or local shops.

Suite – A type of dorm room. Unlike dorms that feature communal bathrooms shared by the entire floor, suites offer bathrooms shared only among the suite. Suite-style dorm rooms can house anywhere from two to ten students.

TA (Teacher's Assistant) – An undergraduate or grad student who helps in some manner with a specific course. In some cases, a TA will teach a class, assist a professor, grade assignments, or conduct office hours.

Undergraduate – A student in the process of studying for his or her bachelor's degree.

ABOUT THE AUTHOR

I'm really excited to have had the opportunity to inform people about USC. As a second-year print journalism major, I take advantage of every chance to get experience writing and improve my skills. Authoring this book has allowed me to do all of this while having fun at the same time! Born in Missouri, but raised in the Southeast, USC was a natural choice for me, considering that I live within a half-hour drive from campus. Little did I know then how many amazing people I would meet here, how many fun experiences I would have, and how much I would learn. Going to USC has been a great adventure for me thus far, and I hope that this book will help others make the college choice that is right for them, whether that college is USC or not.

I would like to give a quick thanks to some important people who have provided me with so much love and support. Thank you Mom, Dad, Lori, Michelle, Donna, Steve, Fred, Cotters, Aunt Carmen, the many teachers who have inspired me along the way to work hard to achieve my goals, and the people at College Prowler for making this all possible.

Jessica Foster
jessicafoster@collegeprowler.com

The College Prowler
Big Book of Colleges

Having Trouble Narrowing Down Your Choices?

Try Going Bigger!

BIG BOOK OF COLLEGES '09
7¼" X 10", 1248 Pages Paperback
$29.95 Retail
978-1-4274-0005-5

Choosing the perfect school can be an overwhelming
challenge. Luckily, our *Big Book of Colleges* makes
that task a little less daunting. We've packed it with
overviews of our full library of single-school guides—
more than 280 of the nation's top schools—giving you
some much-needed perspective on your search.

College Prowler on the Web

Craving some electronic interaction? Check out the new and improved **CollegeProwler.com**! We've included the COMPLETE contents of more than 250 of our single-school guides on the Web—and you can gain access to all of them for just $39.95 per year!

Not only that, but non-subscribers can still view and compare our grades for each school, order books at our online bookstore, or enter our monthly scholarship contest. Don't get left in the dark when making your college decision. Let College Prowler be your guide!

Get the Jolt!

College Jolt gives you a peek behind the scenes

College Jolt is our new blog designed to hook you up with great information, funny videos, cool contests, awesome scholarship opportunities, and honest insight into who we are and what we're all about.

Check us out at ***www.collegejolt.com***

Tell Us What Life Is Really Like at Your School!

Have you ever wanted to let people know what your college is really like? Now's your chance to help millions of high school students choose the right college.

Let your voice be heard.

Check out *www.collegeprowler.com* for more info!

Need More Help?

Do you have more questions about this school? Can't find a certain statistic? College Prowler is here to help. We are the best source of college information out there. We have a network of thousands of students who can get the latest information on any school to you ASAP. E-mail us at info@collegeprowler.com with your college-related questions.

E-Mail Us Your College-Related Questions!

Check out *www.collegeprowler.com* for more details.
1-800-290-2682

Write For Us!

Get published! Voice your opinion.

Writing a College Prowler guidebook is both fun and rewarding; our open-ended format allows your own creativity free reign. Our writers have been featured in national newspapers and have seen their names in bookstores across the country. Now is your chance to break into the publishing industry with one of the country's fastest-growing publishers!

Apply now at **www.collegeprowler.com**

Contact editor@collegeprowler.com or
call 1-800-290-2682 for more details.

Pros and Cons

Still can't figure out if this is the right school for you?
You've already read through this in-depth guide;
why not list the pros and cons? It will really help
with narrowing down your decision and determining
whether or not this school is right for you.

Pros	Cons
....	....
....	....
....	....
....	....
....	....
....	....
....	....
....	....
....	....
....	....
....	....
....	....
....	....

Pros and Cons

Still can't figure out if this is the right school for you?
You've already read through this in-depth guide;
why not list the pros and cons? It will really help
with narrowing down your decision and determining
whether or not this school is right for you.

Pros	Cons
....	....
....	....
....	....
....	....
....	....
....	....
....	....
....	....
....	....
....	....
....	....
....	....
....	....

Notes

....

....

....

....

....

....

....

....

....

....

....

....

....

....

Notes

....

....

....

....

....

....

....

....

....

....

....

....

....

Notes

....

....

....

....

....

....

....

....

....

....

....

....

....

Notes

Notes

Notes

....

....

....

....

....

....

....

....

....

....

....

....

....

Notes

....

....

....

....

....

....

....

....

....

....

....

....

....

Notes

....

....

....

....

....

....

....

....

....

....

....

....

....

Notes

....

....

....

....

....

....

....

....

....

....

....

....

....

Notes

Notes

....

....

....

....

....

....

....

....

....

....

....

....

....

Notes

Notes

....

....

....

....

....

....

....

....

....

....

....

....

....

Notes

Notes

....

....

....

....

....

....

....

....

....

....

....

....

....

Albion College
Alfred University
Allegheny College
American University
Amherst College
Arizona State University
Auburn University
Babson College
Ball State University
Bard College
Barnard College
Bates College
Baylor University
Beloit College
Bentley College
Binghamton University
Birmingham Southern College
Boston College
Boston University
Bowdoin College
Brandeis University
Brigham Young University
Brown University
Bryn Mawr College
Bucknell University
Cal Poly
Cal Poly Pomona
Cal State Northridge
Cal State Sacramento
Caltech
Carleton College
Carnegie Mellon University
Case Western Reserve
Centenary College of Louisiana
Centre College
Claremont McKenna College
Clark Atlanta University
Clark University
Clemson University
Colby College
Colgate University
College of Charleston
College of the Holy Cross
College of William & Mary
College of Wooster
Colorado College
Columbia University
Connecticut College
Cornell University
Creighton University
CUNY Hunters College
Dartmouth College
Davidson College
Denison University
DePauw University
Dickinson College
Drexel University
Duke University
Duquesne University
Earlham College
East Carolina University
Elon University
Emerson College
Emory University
FIT
Florida State University
Fordham University

Franklin & Marshall College
Furman University
Geneva College
George Washington University
Georgetown University
Georgia Tech
Gettysburg College
Gonzaga University
Goucher College
Grinnell College
Grove City College
Guilford College
Gustavus Adolphus College
Hamilton College
Hampshire College
Hampton University
Hanover College
Harvard University
Harvey Mudd College
Haverford College
Hofstra University
Hollins University
Howard University
Idaho State University
Illinois State University
Illinois Wesleyan University
Indiana University
Iowa State University
Ithaca College
IUPUI
James Madison University
Johns Hopkins University
Juniata College
Kansas State
Kent State University
Kenyon College
Lafayette College
LaRoche College
Lawrence University
Lehigh University
Lewis & Clark College
Louisiana State University
Loyola College in Maryland
Loyola Marymount University
Loyola University Chicago
Loyola University New Orleans
Macalester College
Marlboro College
Marquette University
McGill University
Miami University of Ohio
Michigan State University
Middle Tennessee State
Middlebury College
Millsaps College
MIT
Montana State University
Mount Holyoke College
Muhlenberg College
New York University
North Carolina State
Northeastern University
Northern Arizona University
Northern Illinois University
Northwestern University
Oberlin College
Occidental College

Ohio State University
Ohio University
Ohio Wesleyan University
Old Dominion University
Penn State University
Pepperdine University
Pitzer College
Pomona College
Princeton University
Providence College
Purdue University
Reed College
Rensselaer Polytechnic Institute
Rhode Island School of Design
Rhodes College
Rice University
Rochester Institute of Technology
Rollins College
Rutgers University
San Diego State University
Santa Clara University
Sarah Lawrence College
Scripps College
Seattle University
Seton Hall University
Simmons College
Skidmore College
Slippery Rock
Smith College
Southern Methodist University
Southwestern University
Spelman College
St. Joseph's University Philladelphia
St. John's University
St. Louis University
St. Olaf College
Stanford University
Stetson University
Stony Brook University
Susquhanna University
Swarthmore College
Syracuse University
Temple University
Tennessee State University
Texas A & M University
Texas Christian University
Towson University
Trinity College Connecticut
Trinity University Texas
Truman State
Tufts University
Tulane University
UC Berkeley
UC Davis
UC Irvine
UC Riverside
UC San Diego
UC Santa Barbara
UC Santa Cruz
UCLA
Union College
University at Albany
University at Buffalo
University of Alabama
University of Arizona
University of Central Florida
University of Chicago

University of Colorado
University of Connecticut
University of Delaware
University of Denver
University of Florida
University of Georgia
University of Illinois
University of Iowa
University of Kansas
University of Kentucky
University of Maine
University of Maryland
University of Massachusetts
University of Miami
University of Michigan
University of Minnesota
University of Mississippi
University of Missouri
University of Nebraska
University of New Hampshire
University of North Carolina
University of Notre Dame
University of Oklahoma
University of Oregon
University of Pennsylvania
University of Pittsburgh
University of Puget Sound
University of Rhode Island
University of Richmond
University of Rochester
University of San Diego
University of San Francisco
University of South Carolina
University of South Dakota
University of South Florida
University of Southern California
University of Tennessee
University of Texas
University of Utah
University of Vermont
University of Virginia
University of Washington
University of Wisconsin
UNLV
Ursinus College
Valparaiso University
Vanderbilt University
Vassar College
Villanova University
Virginia Tech
Wake Forest University
Warren Wilson College
Washington and Lee University
Washington University in St. Louis
Wellesley College
Wesleyan University
West Point
West Virginia University
Wheaton College IL
Wheaton College MA
Whitman College
Wilkes University
Williams College
Xavier University
Yale University

Made in the USA
Lexington, KY
16 March 2011